MW00896820

HAWAII BUCKET LIST

Set Off on **120 Epic Adventures** and Discover
Incredible Destinations to Live Out Your Dreams
While Creating Unforgettable Memories
that Will Last a Lifetime.

*(Online Digital MAP included - access it through
the link provided in the MAP Chapter of this book)*

BeCrePress Travel

© **Copyright 2024 by BeCrePress Travel—All rights reserved**.

This document is geared towards providing exact and reliable information regarding the topic and issue covered.

From a Declaration of Principles which was accepted and approved equally by a Committee of the American Bar Association and a Committee of Publishers and Associations.

In no way is it legal to reproduce, duplicate, or transmit any part of this document in either electronic means or in printed format. All rights reserved.

The information provided herein is stated to be truthful and consistent, in that any liability, in terms of inattention or otherwise, by any usage or abuse of any policies, processes, or directions contained within is the solitary and utter responsibility of the recipient reader. Under no circumstances will any legal responsibility or blame be held against the publisher for any reparation, damages, or monetary loss due to the information herein, either directly or indirectly.

Respective authors own all copyrights not held by the publisher.

The information herein is offered for informational purposes solely and is universal as so. The presentation of the information is without a contract or any type of guarantee assurance.

The trademarks that are used are without any consent, and the publication of the trademark is without permission or backing by the trademark owner. All trademarks and brands within this book are for clarifying purposes only and are owned by the owners themselves, not affiliated with this document.

HAWAII BUCKET LIST

TABLE OF CONTENTS

HAWAII BUCKET LIST

INTRODUCTION

Get ready to dive into paradise with *Hawaii Bucket List: Set Off on 120 Epic Adventures and Discover Incredible Destinations to Live Out Your Dreams.* Whether you've always imagined yourself lounging on sun-kissed beaches, hiking through lush rainforests, or exploring the rich history of the Hawaiian Islands, this guide will ignite your wanderlust and inspire you to live out the ultimate island adventure. Hawaii's beauty is unparalleled, from its volcanic landscapes to its pristine shores—and with this book, you'll discover the very best of it, one breathtaking destination at a time.

Imagine standing at the edge of Waimea Canyon, the "Grand Canyon of the Pacific," with its vibrant colors and dramatic cliffs. Picture yourself at the summit of Haleakalā Crater, watching the sun rise over a sea of clouds, or snorkeling in the crystal-clear waters of Hanauma Bay, surrounded by tropical fish. This book is your invitation to explore, to dream, and to experience Hawaii like never before. From iconic surf spots like Banzai Pipeline and Sunset Beach to hidden gems like the serene Byodo-In Temple and the awe-inspiring Rainbow Falls, Hawaii's treasures await you.

Each destination in this guide is carefully curated to ensure that your journey is not only exciting but also hassle-free. You'll find:

- **A detailed description** of the destination that paints a vivid picture, immersing you in the natural beauty, culture, or adventure that awaits.

- **The exact address** so there's no confusion about where you're heading, whether you're off to explore historic Iolani Palace or take in the stunning views at Pololu Valley Lookout.

- **The nearest city** to give you context and help you plan your travels with ease, ensuring you know just how far your next adventure is from your current stop.

- **GPS coordinates** are ready to be plugged into your navigation system, allowing you to get where you need to go with zero stress.

- **The best time to visit** each destination, so you'll know when to go for the perfect weather, optimal views, or seasonal events. No more guessing—you'll be fully prepared to experience each destination at its finest.

- **Tolls and access fees** are listed, so you won't be caught off guard. Whether it's a small parking fee at a beach park or a toll along a scenic drive, you'll have all the information you need up front.

- **A fun fact or trivia** about the destination will spark your curiosity and add a layer of depth to your visit. Whether it's learning about the rich history of Pu'uhonua O Hōnaunau National Historical Park or discovering a fascinating tidbit about the volcanic forces that shaped Hawaii Volcanoes National Park, you'll leave each place with a story to tell.

- **Website** links are provided to keep you up to date on everything from hours of operation to special events, ensuring your visit is seamless and full of opportunity.

And, as a special bonus, we've included an **interactive State Map** that's pre-loaded with all 120 destinations! Forget wasting time trying to figure out where each place is—this digital map will be your trusted companion, guiding you from one epic spot to the next without any frustration or confusion.

Hawaii is more than just a collection of beautiful islands—it's a place where adventure meets serenity, where history and culture blend effortlessly with nature's raw beauty. Whether you're standing on the black sands of Punalu'u Beach, marveling at the power of the Halona Blowhole, or walking through the lush Hoomaluhia Botanical Gardens, you'll experience moments that will forever live in your heart.

This guide is designed to help you uncover the magic of Hawaii, whether you're a first-time visitor or a seasoned explorer.

From the towering waterfalls of Akaka Falls State Park to the tranquil shores of Turtle Bay Beach, Hawaii's beauty is limitless, and this book will guide you to the very best of it. Each page is packed with tips, insider knowledge, and must-see sights, all aimed at making your Hawaiian adventure as incredible as it can be.

So, are you ready to set off on 120 epic adventures? Whether you're hiking the Pipiwai Trail to its bamboo forest and cascading waterfalls or enjoying a quiet moment at the USS Arizona Memorial, this guide will take you on a journey that promises to create memories to last a lifetime. The islands are calling, and there's no better time to answer. Your Hawaiian dreams are just a page away—let's get started!

ABOUT HAWAII

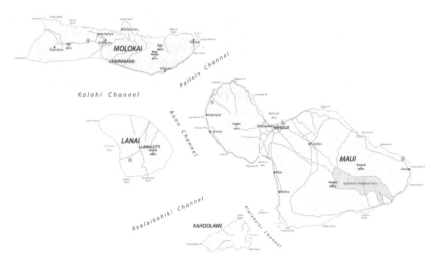

To access the Digital Map, please refer to the 'Map Chapter' in this book

Landscape of Hawaii

Hawaii's landscape is nothing short of a tropical paradise, a breathtaking symphony of nature that blends fiery volcanoes, lush rainforests, and pristine beaches into a world unlike any other. Born from the depths of the Pacific Ocean, the Hawaiian Islands are a geological wonder, shaped by powerful volcanic forces that continue to sculpt the land today. The towering volcanoes, like Mauna Kea and Kīlauea, offer a raw, untamed beauty, where you can witness molten lava slowly forging new land or hike through ancient lava tubes. These active volcanoes, nestled within Hawaii Volcanoes National Park, serve as a powerful reminder of the ever-changing nature of these islands.

Imagine standing at the edge of Haleakalā Crater, gazing at the otherworldly landscape that seems to stretch endlessly toward the sky, or driving along the scenic Chain of Craters Road, where black lava fields meet the sparkling Pacific Ocean in a stunning contrast of textures and colors. The dramatic cliffs of the Nā Pali Coast rise like emerald green giants above the ocean, while the majestic Waimea

Canyon, often called the "Grand Canyon of the Pacific," carves through the landscape with vibrant layers of red, orange, and green.

Hawaii's beaches are legendary, from the golden sands of Ka'anapali Beach to the jet-black shores of Punalu'u Black Sand Beach. The sea meets the land in brilliant displays, like the turquoise waters of Lanikai Beach or the crashing waves at Waimea Bay, famous for its epic surf. Hidden waterfalls, like those found along the Hana Highway or cascading down in Akaka Falls State Park, add to the state's dreamlike charm.

From the heights of Mauna Kea Summit, where stargazing feels like touching the heavens, to the lush tropical valleys of the Big Island, Hawaii's landscape is an invitation to explore a world where nature reigns supreme. This is a place where adventure awaits around every corner, and the land itself tells stories of creation, beauty, and wonder.

Flora and Fauna of Hawaii

Hawaii's flora and fauna are a reflection of its unique, isolated location in the middle of the Pacific Ocean, creating a lush paradise where plant and animal life thrive in diverse ecosystems. Imagine towering rainforests dripping with ferns, ancient trees, and brightly colored tropical flowers, while misty waterfalls cascade down volcanic cliffs. The Hawaiian Islands are home to an incredible array of plants, many of which are found nowhere else in the world. As you hike along trails like the Pipiwai Trail near Haleakalā Crater or explore the valleys of Waimea Canyon, you'll encounter vibrant hibiscus, delicate orchids, and the endemic 'ōhi'a lehua tree, whose fiery red blossoms add a splash of color to the landscape.

The flora of Hawaii ranges from the dense, verdant rainforests filled with coconut palms, banyan trees, and fragrant plumeria to the windswept, arid coastal areas dotted with hardy naupaka shrubs and pandanus trees. These ecosystems, though diverse, are fragile, and many plants are carefully preserved in botanical gardens like Lyon Arboretum or the Hawaii Tropical Botanical Garden, where you can explore native species and rare tropical wonders alike.

Hawaii's fauna is just as extraordinary. Picture swimming alongside graceful sea turtles in the crystal-clear waters of Turtle Bay Beach or witnessing the playful antics of spinner dolphins off the coast of Kailua Beach. The islands' surrounding coral reefs, like those in Hanauma Bay, are bustling with marine life, from vibrant parrotfish to the elusive Hawaiian monk seal. On land, you may catch sight of the majestic pueo, Hawaii's native owl, soaring through the skies or hear the melodious songs of the nēnē, the state's beloved goose, as you hike through its natural habitats.

Hawaii's delicate balance of rare and exotic flora and fauna makes it a living sanctuary, offering endless opportunities to connect with nature in its purest, most awe-inspiring form.

Climate of Hawaii

Hawaii's climate is nothing short of paradise, a warm, tropical dream that invites you to explore its beauty year-round. With temperatures averaging between 75°F and 85°F (24°C to 29°C) throughout the year, every day in Hawaii feels like the perfect day for an adventure. Imagine the gentle ocean breezes cooling your skin as you stroll along the golden sands of Waikiki Beach or the refreshing mist that kisses your face as you hike through the lush rainforests of Waipio Valley. The islands experience two primary seasons: a warmer, drier summer from May to October and a slightly cooler, wetter winter from November to April, but even in the rain, Hawaii's magic is ever-present.

In the summer months, the beaches beckon with crystal-clear waters, ideal for snorkeling at Hanauma Bay or watching sea turtles at Turtle Bay Beach. Trade winds bring a refreshing breeze that sweeps across the islands, making the heat feel just right. Winter brings a slightly cooler touch to the air, perfect for exploring the majestic peaks of Mauna Kea Summit or marveling at the powerful waves crashing on Oahu's North Shore at Waimea Bay, famous for its world-class surfing conditions.

Hawaii's unique microclimates ensure that no matter where you go, there's always something extraordinary to experience. From the cool, crisp air atop Haleakalā Crater to the tropical humidity of the rainforests around Akaka Falls, the islands are a patchwork of diverse environments that cater to every traveler's desire. The leeward sides of the islands offer sun-drenched beaches, while the windward sides receive more rain, creating lush, green landscapes filled with waterfalls and vibrant plant life.

Whether you're chasing the sun on Lanikai Beach or enjoying the misty charm of Waimea Canyon, Hawaii's climate ensures that every day is filled with adventure and natural beauty. It's a place where the weather is as inviting as the landscape, drawing you in to explore, relax, and fall in love with the islands.

History of Hawaii

Hawaii's history is as rich and captivating as its stunning landscapes, a tale that stretches across centuries and cultures, intertwining the stories of Polynesian voyagers, mighty kings, and global powers. Imagine the first Polynesian settlers arriving by canoe over 1,500 years ago, guided only by the stars and the ocean's currents. These early explorers, thought to have come from the Marquesas and Tahiti, established the first human presence on the islands, bringing with them their deep connection to the land, ocean, and skies, which still influences Hawaiian culture today.

For centuries, the Hawaiian Islands were a collection of independent chiefdoms, each ruled by powerful ali'i (chiefs) who governed over their territories. The Polynesian people cultivated the fertile lands, creating sophisticated agricultural systems and developing a society deeply rooted in spirituality and respect for nature. Ancient Hawaiians believed the islands were the physical embodiment of their gods, and their cultural practices, like hula and chants, connected them to their ancestors and the forces of nature.

One of the most dramatic shifts in Hawaiian history came with the rise of King Kamehameha I, known as the Napoleon of the Pacific. Born in the 18th century, Kamehameha rose to power and became the first to unify all the Hawaiian Islands under one kingdom by 1810. His legacy can be felt throughout Hawaii, with statues like the one in downtown Honolulu serving as reminders of his powerful reign. The unification of the islands brought an era of peace and allowed Hawaii to flourish, with trade routes expanding and international relationships developing.

However, this newfound unity was soon tested by the arrival of Western explorers. In 1778, British Captain James Cook became the first European to make contact with the Hawaiian Islands, forever changing the course of Hawaii's history. While Cook's arrival was initially met with curiosity and hospitality, it also marked the beginning of significant changes for the islands, including the introduction of new diseases that devastated the native population. Cook's death in 1779 at Kealakekua Bay is immortalized by the Captain Cook Monument, a reminder of the complex and often tumultuous interactions between Hawaiians and Westerners.

As Western influence grew, so did Hawaii's role on the global stage. Missionaries arrived in the early 19th century, bringing Christianity and introducing a written Hawaiian language, which helped to preserve many of the islands' ancient stories and traditions. At the same time, sugarcane and pineapple plantations transformed the economic landscape, drawing immigrants from China, Japan, Portugal, and the Philippines, who arrived to work on the plantations. This influx of cultures would shape Hawaii's multicultural identity, one of its most unique characteristics today.

The 19th century also saw the construction of significant landmarks like Iolani Palace, the only royal palace in the United States, which stands in Honolulu as a symbol of Hawaii's monarchical past. King Kalākaua, known as the "Merrie Monarch," and his sister, Queen Lili'uokalani, the last reigning monarch of Hawaii, fought to preserve Hawaiian sovereignty during a time of increasing American influence. However, in 1893, Queen Lili'uokalani was overthrown in a coup led by American and European businessmen, setting the stage for Hawaii's eventual annexation by the United States in 1898.

The transition from a monarchy to a U.S. territory was bittersweet for the Hawaiian people, but it didn't erase the pride they held in their culture and traditions. Even as Hawaii became a strategic U.S. territory, known for its sugar exports and military significance, the aloha spirit—marked by warmth, kindness, and hospitality—remained a defining feature of the islands.

This spirit would be tested again in the 20th century, most notably on December 7, 1941, when Pearl Harbor was attacked by Japanese forces, drawing the United States into World War II. Today, visitors can pay tribute to this somber chapter of Hawaii's history at the USS Arizona Memorial, a poignant reminder of the sacrifices made during the war.

Despite these challenges, Hawaii continued to grow, and in 1959, it officially became the 50th state of the United States. This momentous occasion ushered in a new era of prosperity and development, as Hawaii became a destination known around the world for its natural beauty and rich cultural heritage. Landmarks like the Bishop Museum and the Honolulu Museum of Art preserve and celebrate Hawaii's vibrant past, while sites like the Polynesian Cultural Center and Pu'uhonua O Hōnaunau National Historical Park offer a glimpse into ancient Hawaiian life and traditions.

But Hawaii's history isn't just about kings and conflicts—it's about the everyday people who have made these islands their home for generations. The sugarcane fields may have disappeared, but the spirit of aloha thrives in the local communities, where Hawaiian culture is passed down through hula, music, language, and the reverence for nature. Whether you're strolling through the lush gardens of Hoomaluhia Botanical Gardens or gazing at the mighty Mauna Kea Summit, you're walking in the footsteps of those who have long cherished and protected this land.

As you explore Hawaii's rich history, from the ancient petroglyphs along the Kīlauea Iki Trail to the royal palaces and WWII memorials, you'll uncover a story filled with resilience, pride, and aloha. This is a place where the past and present live side by side, where every wave that crashes on the shore and every breeze that sweeps through the valleys carries with it the echoes of Hawaii's storied past. Whether you're admiring the powerful legacy of King Kamehameha or reflecting on the sacrifices at Pearl Harbor, Hawaii's history will touch your heart and deepen your appreciation for the islands' beauty and spirit.

Hawaii's journey from an ancient Polynesian kingdom to the multicultural paradise we know today is a testament to the strength of its people and the enduring power of its culture. As you explore its historical landmarks, you'll find that every corner of these islands tells a story—stories of kings and queens, explorers and warriors, immigrants and locals, all woven into the fabric of this extraordinary place. And through it all, the spirit of aloha—rooted in love, respect, and kindness—remains at the heart of Hawaii's history, inviting visitors to experience the islands' past and present in a way that is both deeply meaningful and endlessly inspiring.

HOW TO USE THIS GUIDE

Welcome to your comprehensive guide to exploring Hawaii! This chapter is dedicated to helping you understand how to effectively use this guide and the interactive map to enhance your travel experience. Let's dive into the simple steps to navigate the book and utilize the digital tools provided, ensuring you have the best adventure possible.

Understanding the Guide's Structure

The guide features 120 of the best destinations across the beautiful state of Hawaii, thoughtfully compiled to inspire and facilitate your explorations. These destinations are divided into areas and listed alphabetically. This organization aims to simplify your search process, making it quick and intuitive to locate each destination in the book.

Using the Alphabetical Listings

Since the destination areas are arranged alphabetically, you can easily flip through the guide to find a specific place or browse areas that catch your interest. Each destination entry in the book includes essential information such as:

- A vivid description of the destination.

- The complete address and the nearest major city, giving you a quick geographical context.

- GPS coordinates for precise navigation.

- The best times to visit, helping you plan your trip according to seasonal attractions and weather.

- Details on tolls or access fees, preparing you for any costs associated with your visit.

- Fun trivia to enhance your knowledge and appreciation of each location.

- A link to the official website for up-to-date information.

To further enhance your experience and save time, you can scan these website links using apps like Google Lens to open them directly without the need to type them into a browser. This seamless integration allows for quicker access to the latest information and resources about each destination.

Navigating with the Interactive State Map

Your guide comes equipped with an innovative tool—an interactive map of Hawaii that integrates seamlessly with Google Maps. This digital map is pre-loaded with all 120 destinations, offering an effortless way to visualize and plan your journey across the state.

How to Use the Map:

- **Open the Interactive Map**: Start by accessing the digital map through the link provided in your guide. You can open it on any device that supports Google Maps, such as a smartphone, tablet, or computer.

- **Choose Your Starting Point:** Decide where you will begin your adventure. You might start from your current location or another specific point in Hawaii.

- **Explore Nearby Destinations:** With the map open, zoom in and out to view the destinations near your starting point. Click on any marker to see a brief description and access quick links for navigation and more details.

- **Plan Your Itinerary:** Based on the destinations close to your chosen start, you can create a personalized itinerary. You can select multiple locations to visit in a day or plan a more extended road trip through various regions.

Combining the Book and Map for Best Results

To get the most out of your adventures:

- Cross-Reference: Use the interactive map to spot destinations you are interested in and then refer back to the guidebook for detailed information and insights.

- Plan Sequentially: As you plan your route on the map, use the alphabetical listing in the book to easily gather information on each destination and organize your visits efficiently.

- Stay Updated: Regularly check the provided website links for any changes in operation hours, fees, or special events at the destinations.

By following these guidelines and utilizing both the guidebook and the interactive map, you will be well-equipped to explore Hawaii's diverse landscapes and attractions.

Whether you are seeking solitude in nature, adventure in the outdoors, or cultural experiences in urban settings, this guide will serve as your reliable companion, ensuring every adventure is memorable and every discovery is enriching. Happy travels!

ISLAND OF HAWAII

CAPTAIN COOK

Kealakekua Bay

Immerse yourself in the stunning beauty of Kealakekua Bay, located in Captain Cook on the Island of Hawaii. This serene bay is a treasure trove of marine life, offering visitors unparalleled opportunities for snorkeling and kayaking amidst vibrant coral reefs. The historical significance of the bay, being the landing site of Captain James Cook in 1779, adds a layer of intrigue to the natural beauty. Explore the underwater wonders, spot dolphins playing in the distance, and learn about the cultural heritage that makes Kealakekua Bay a must-visit destination.

Location: Kealakekua Bay, Captain Cook, Island of Hawaii, HI 96704

Closest City or Town: Captain Cook, Hawaii

How to Get There: From Kailua-Kona, take HI-11 south to Kealakekua Bay. Follow Napoopoo Road to the bay.

GPS Coordinates: 19.4782437° N, 155.9259272° W

Best Time to Visit: Early morning for calm waters and fewer crowds.

Pass/Permit/Fees: Free to visit; fees apply for guided tours and rentals.

Did You Know? Kealakekua Bay is a Marine Life Conservation District, ensuring the protection of its pristine reefs and diverse marine species.

Website: http://www.lovebigisland.com/kealakekua-bay/

The Captain Cook Monument

Embark on a journey through history at The Captain Cook Monument, located at Kealakekua Bay in Captain Cook on the Island of Hawaii. This towering obelisk marks the spot where British explorer Captain

James Cook met his end in 1779. Accessible primarily by boat or a challenging hike, the monument offers stunning views of the bay and serves as a significant historical site. Visitors can pay their respects and learn about Cook's voyages while enjoying the panoramic scenery and abundant marine life in the surrounding waters.

Location: Kealakekua Bay, Captain Cook, Island of Hawaii, HI 96704

Closest City or Town: Captain Cook, Hawaii

How to Get There: From Kailua-Kona, take HI-11 south. Park at Napoopoo Road and hike or kayak to the monument.

GPS Coordinates: 19.4813011° N, 155.9334285° W

Best Time to Visit: Morning for cooler temperatures and calm seas.

Pass/Permit/Fees: Free to visit; guided tours available at additional cost.

Did You Know? The Captain Cook Monument was erected by the British in 1874, and the land it stands on is still considered British territory.

Website: http://www.gohawaii.com/en/big-island/regions-neighborhoods/kona/kealakekua-bay

HAWAII VOLCANOES NATIONAL PARK

Hawaii Volcanoes National Park

Find your sense of wonder and excitement at Hawaii Volcanoes National Park, a geological marvel located on the Big Island of Hawaii. Home to two of the world's most active volcanoes, Kīlauea and Mauna Loa, this park offers an unparalleled glimpse into the fiery forces that shape our planet. Located in the heart of the island, visitors can hike through volcanic craters, walk on hardened lava flows, and witness the glowing lava lakes. The park's unique feature is its dynamic volcanic landscape, providing an ever-changing canvas of geological activity and natural beauty.

Location: Volcano National Park, Hawaii Volcanoes National Park, Island of Hawaii, HI 96785

Closest City or Town: Hilo, Island of Hawaii, HI

How to Get There: From Hilo, take the HI-11 S (Hawaii Belt Road) to the park entrance.

GPS Coordinates: 19.4290543° N, 155.2568892° W

Best Time to Visit: Year-round, but winter offers cooler weather for hiking.

Pass/Permit/Fees: Entrance fee: $30 per vehicle.

Did You Know? Kīlauea is one of the most active volcanoes in the world, with continuous eruptions occurring since 1983 until recently.

Website: http://www.nps.gov/havo

Kīlauea Iki Trail

Find your sense of adventure on the Kīlauea Iki Trail, located within the awe-inspiring Hawaii Volcanoes National Park. This exhilarating hike takes you through the lush jungle and descends into the volcanic crater, offering an up-close experience with the remnants of a massive 1959 eruption. You'll traverse hardened lava fields, steam vents, and towering walls of the crater, capturing the raw power of volcanic activity. The unique feature of Kīlauea Iki Trail is the surreal feeling of walking on solidified lava, a stark contrast to the surrounding verdant landscape.

Location: Crater Rim Drive, Hawaii Volcanoes National Park, Island of Hawaii, HI 96785

Closest City or Town: Hilo, Hawaii

How to Get There: From Hilo, take Highway 11 south to the entrance of Hawaii Volcanoes National Park, then follow Crater Rim Drive to the Kīlauea Iki parking area.

GPS Coordinates: 19.4136188° N, 155.2387526° W

Best Time to Visit: Early morning or late afternoon to avoid the midday heat.

Pass/Permit/Fees: Park entry fee required; visit the park's official website for current rates.

Did You Know? The Kīlauea Iki eruption of 1959 saw lava fountains reaching up to 1,900 feet high, making it one of Hawaii's most spectacular eruptions.

Website: https://noahlangphotography.com/blog/kilauea-iki-trail-hawaii-volcanoes-national-park

HILO

Akaka Falls State Park

Discover the breathtaking beauty of Akaka Falls State Park, home to one of Hawaii's most spectacular waterfalls. Located in the lush region of Honomu on the Island of Hawaii, this park invites you to immerse yourself in its tropical splendor as you walk along a paved path through dense rainforest. The highlight of this adventure is the stunning 442-foot Akaka Falls, which cascades into a deep gorge. Visitors can also admire the nearby Kahuna Falls and the vibrant flora that surrounds these natural wonders.

Location: VR3X+P5, 875 Akaka Falls Rd, Honomu, HI 96728

Closest City or Town: Hilo, Hawaii

How to Get There: From Hilo, head north on Highway 19, turn onto Akaka Falls Road, and follow the signs to the park.

GPS Coordinates: 19.8542629° N, 155.1521154° W

Best Time to Visit: Morning to mid-afternoon for the best lighting and to avoid potential rainy weather.

Pass/Permit/Fees: Entry fee required; visit the park's website for more details.

Did You Know? Akaka Falls gets its name from the Hawaiian word 'ākaka, which means split or crack, describing the way it seems to split the gorge.

Website: http://dlnr.hawaii.gov/dsp/parks/hawaii/akaka-falls-state-park/

Imiloa Astronomy Center

Delve into the wonders of the universe at the Imiloa Astronomy Center, located in Hilo on the Island of Hawaii. This state-of-the-art facility marries Hawaiian culture with cutting-edge astronomy, offering interactive exhibits and an immersive planetarium. Visitors can explore the cosmic phenomena through presentations and hands-on displays that illustrate the connections between ancient

Polynesian navigation and modern astronomical research. The Imiloa Astronomy Center is unique for showcasing how Hawaii's volcanic peaks provide an unparalleled vantage point for observing the stars.

Location: 600 Imiloa Pl, Hilo, Island of Hawaii, HI 96720-4072

Closest City or Town: Hilo, Hawaii

How to Get There: From Hilo, take Komohana Street to Nowelo Street, and follow signs to the Imiloa Astronomy Center.

GPS Coordinates: 19.7011173° N, 155.0886773° W

Best Time to Visit: Year-round, with daily shows at various times; check the schedule online.

Pass/Permit/Fees: Admission fees apply; see the website for details.

Did You Know? The center's name, 'Imiloa," means "to explore new knowledge in Hawaiian, reflecting its mission to blend indigenous wisdom with scientific discovery.

Website: http://www.imiloahawaii.org/

Pacific Tsunami Museum

Explore the powerful history and science of tsunamis at the Pacific Tsunami Museum in Hilo, Hawaii. Situated on the Island of Hawaii, this museum offers compelling exhibits that recount the devastating tsunamis that have struck the Hawaiian Islands. Learn about the local and global impact of these natural disasters through personal stories, interactive displays, and scientific explanations. The museum serves as both a remembrance of past events and an educational resource for tsunami preparedness.

Location: 130 Kamehameha Ave, Hilo, Island of Hawaii, HI 96720-2833

Closest City or Town: Hilo, Hawaii

How to Get There: From downtown Hilo, head east on Kamehameha Avenue; the museum is located near the waterfront.

GPS Coordinates: 19.7259466° N, 155.0866304° W

Best Time to Visit: Open year-round; weekdays are less crowded.

Pass/Permit/Fees: Admission fees apply; see the website for current rates.

Did You Know? The museum is housed in a historic building that survived the devastating 1946 tsunami in Hilo.

Website: http://tsunami.org/

Panaewa Rainforest Zoo and Gardens

Immerse yourself in the tropical beauty and wildlife diversity at Panaewa Rainforest Zoo and Gardens in Hilo on the Island of Hawaii. This unique zoo is set within a lush rainforest and is home to over 100 animal species, including native Hawaiian fauna and exotic creatures. Wander through botanical gardens that feature vibrant orchids, bamboos, and tropical plants. One of the highlights is meeting Namaste, the zoo's white Bengal tiger, and exploring the children's petting zoo for a hands-on experience.

Location: 800 Stainback Hwy, Hilo, Island of Hawaii, HI 96720

Closest City or Town: Hilo, Hawaii

How to Get There: From Hilo, take Highway 11 south to Stainback Highway, and follow signs to the zoo.

GPS Coordinates: 19.6542357° N, 155.0727822° W

Best Time to Visit: Morning hours when animals are most active.

Pass/Permit/Fees: Free admission; donations are welcomed.

Did You Know? Panaewa Rainforest Zoo is the only tropical rainforest zoo in the United States.

Website: http://www.hilozoo.org/

Pepeekeo Scenic Drive

Embark on a picturesque journey along the Pepeekeo Scenic Drive, a 4-mile route nestled near Pepeekeo on the Island of Hawaii. Known for its lush greenery, cascading waterfalls, and ocean vistas, this drive offers a tranquil escape into nature's splendor. Meandering through dense rainforests, you'll encounter vibrant local flora and fauna, along with breathtaking coastal views. This drive is a unique invitation to immerse yourself in the lush beauty of Hawaii's verdant landscapes.

Location: 28-1084 Mamalahoa Hwy, Pepeekeo, HI 96783

Closest City or Town: Hilo, Hawaii

How to Get There: From Hilo, take the Hawaii Belt Road (Highway 19) north for about 8 miles to the turnoff for Pepeekeo Scenic Drive.

GPS Coordinates: 19.8395406° N, 155.1034113° W

Best Time to Visit: Morning to early afternoon for the best light and fewer clouds.

Pass/Permit/Fees: Free to visit.

Did You Know? This drive encompasses part of the Old Mamalahoa Highway, a historic route that connects travelers to the enchanting beauty of Hawaii's countryside.

Website: http://www.instanthawaii.com/cgi-bin/hi?Drives.onomea

Rainbow Falls

Discover the awe-inspiring beauty of Rainbow Falls, located just outside of Hilo on the Island of Hawaii. This remarkable natural wonder plunges 80 feet into a wide pool below, often creating mesmerizing rainbows in the mist. Surrounded by lush rainforest, visitors can explore scenic viewpoints and walking trails to experience the serene power and stunning beauty of the falls up close.

Location: Rainbow Drive, Hilo, Island of Hawaii, HI 96720

Closest City or Town: Hilo, Hawaii

How to Get There: From Hilo, head west on Waianuenue Avenue, follow it until it becomes Rainbow Drive, and continue to the falls parking area.

GPS Coordinates: 19.7184078° N, 155.1089002° W

Best Time to Visit: Morning hours when the sunlight creates rainbows in the mist.

Pass/Permit/Fees: Free to visit.

Did You Know? Rainbow Falls is part of the Wailuku River State Park, which is the longest river in the Hawaiian Islands.

Website: https://dlnr.hawaii.gov/dsp/parks/hawaii/wailuku-river-state-park/

HOLUALOA

Heavenly Hawaiian Kona Coffee Farm Tours & Konalani Coffee Bar

Experience the essence of Kona's coffee culture at Heavenly Hawaiian Kona Coffee Farm, situated in Holualoa on the Island of Hawaii. Explore the lush coffee orchards, learn about the art of coffee growing and processing, and savor freshly brewed Kona coffee at the Konalani Coffee Bar. This immersive tour is perfect for coffee aficionados and those seeking to discover the rich flavors and heritage of Hawaiian coffee.

Location: 78-1136 Bishop Rd, Holualoa, Island of Hawaii, HI 96725-9748

Closest City or Town: Holualoa, Hawaii

How to Get There: From Kailua-Kona, drive south on Highway 11, turn right on Bishop Rd, and follow the signs to the farm.

GPS Coordinates: 19.5559435° N, 155.9298178° W

Best Time to Visit: Morning to early afternoon for tours and fresh coffee tastings.

Pass/Permit/Fees: Tour fees apply; visit their website for current rates.

Did You Know? Kona coffee is known for its rich, smooth flavor, and Heavenly Hawaiian Farm has been cultivating it on volcanic soil for over two decades.

Website: http://heavenlyhawaiian.com/

Hula Daddy Kona Coffee

Delight in the exquisite flavors of Hula Daddy Kona Coffee, a boutique coffee farm located in Holualoa on the Island of Hawaii. Visitors can take a guided tour through the farm's coffee plantations, witness the coffee-making process, and enjoy tastings of their award-winning brews. This destination combines the natural beauty of Kona's volcanic landscape with a deep appreciation for fine coffee.

Location: 74-4944 Mamalahoa Hwy, Holualoa, Island of Hawaii, HI 96725-9604

Closest City or Town: Holualoa, Hawaii

How to Get There: From Kailua-Kona, drive north on Mamalahoa Highway (Highway 180) and follow the signs to Hula Daddy Kona Coffee.

GPS Coordinates: 19.6798923° N, 155.9702264° W

Best Time to Visit: Morning to early afternoon for guided tours and fresh coffee tastings.

Pass/Permit/Fees: Tour fees apply; visit their website for current rates.

Did You Know? Hula Daddy's coffee has been ranked among the top ten coffees in the world and is cultivated on the nutrient-rich slopes of Mauna Loa.

Website: http://www.huladaddy.com/cmd.php?ad=1001960

HONAUNAU

Pu'uhonua O Hōnaunau National Historical Park

Step into Hawaiian history at Pu'uhonua O Hōnaunau National Historical Park, located on the Island of Hawaii. This sacred site once served as a place of refuge for ancient Hawaiians who broke kapu (sacred laws). Explore the historic royal grounds, intricate carvings, and traditional Hawaiian structures that tell stories of a time long past. The park, set against a backdrop of lush greenery and ocean views, offers a unique glimpse into Hawaii's cultural heritage.

Location: State Hwy 160, Honaunau, Island of Hawaii, HI 96726

Closest City or Town: Honaunau, Hawaii

How to Get There: From Kailua-Kona, take Highway 11 south, turn right onto Highway 160, and follow it to the park entrance.

GPS Coordinates: 19.4087958° N, 155.9026125° W

Best Time to Visit: Morning to early afternoon to explore the historical sites and enjoy cooler temperatures.

Pass/Permit/Fees: Entrance fee applies; visit their website for current rates.

Did You Know? Pu'uhonua O Hōnaunau translates to "Place of Refuge at Hōnaunau," and is one of the most important cultural and historical landmarks in Hawaii.

Website: https://www.nps.gov/puho/index.htm

HONOKAA

Waipio Valley Lookout

Find your sense of wonder and serenity at Waipio Valley Lookout, an idyllic destination located on the Island of Hawaii. Perched on the edge of a dramatic cliff, this lookout offers panoramic views of lush, cascading waterfalls, verdant taro fields, and the shimmering black sand beach below. Located on Waipio Valley Road in Honokaa, this spot is a haven for nature lovers and photographers. Take in the breathtaking scenery, enjoy a peaceful hike along the valley's edge, or simply bask in the majesty of the landscape that has inspired countless hearts and minds.

Location: 48-5546 Waipio Valley Rd, Honokaa, Island of Hawaii, HI 96743

Closest City or Town: Honokaa, Hawaii

How to Get There: From Honokaa, take Highway 240 east to the end of the road. The lookout is well-signposted and has a dedicated parking area.

GPS Coordinates: 20.1180193° N, 155.5843480° W

Best Time to Visit: Early morning for the sunrise or late afternoon for a serene sunset experience.

Pass/Permit/Fees: Free to visit.

Did You Know? Waipio Valley is often called the Valley of the Kings due to its historical importance to Hawaiian royalty.

Website: http://www.lovebigisland.com/waipio-valley/#overlook

ISLANDHAWAII

Chain of Craters Road

Embark on a scenic and thrilling journey along Chain of Craters Road, winding through the diverse landscapes of Hawaii Volcanoes National Park on the Island of Hawaii. This route takes you from lush rainforests to barren lava fields, showcasing the raw beauty of volcanic activity. You'll encounter stark contrasts and awe-inspiring geological formations, with opportunities to hike, explore ancient petroglyphs, and view active lava flows. This 19-mile drive is an unforgettable adventure through one of the planet's most dynamic environments.

Location: 8RG4+RW Pahoa, Hawaii

Closest City or Town: Pahoa, Hawaii

How to Get There: From Hilo, take HI-11 to Hawaii Volcanoes National Park, then follow the signs to Chain of Craters Road.

GPS Coordinates: 19.3283608° N, 155.1855720° W

Best Time to Visit: Morning to early afternoon for clear skies and cooler temperatures.

Pass/Permit/Fees: Park entrance fee applies.

Did You Know? Chain of Craters Road was partially covered by lava flows from Kīlauea's ongoing eruption, making it a vivid living example of the island's constant transformation.

Website: http://www.nps.gov/havo/planyourvisit/ccr_tour.htm

Pololu Valley Lookout

Feel the magic of Hawaii's wild beauty at Pololu Valley Lookout, a breathtaking viewpoint located on the Island of Hawaii's northern coast. This lookout offers stunning views of lush, dramatic cliffs, rolling green hills, and the pristine black sand beach below. Adventurous visitors can hike down to the valley floor to immerse themselves in the tranquil and untouched natural scenery. The lookout, positioned at the end of the scenic Akoni Pule Highway, is the perfect spot for nature photography, picnics, and peaceful contemplation.

Location: 52-5100 Akoni Pule Hwy, Island of Hawaii, HI 96755

Closest City or Town: Kapaau, Hawaii

How to Get There: From Waimea, take HI-250 north, then turn left onto Akoni Pule Highway. Follow the road to the end where the lookout is located.

GPS Coordinates: 20.2035807° N, 155.7338497° W

Best Time to Visit: Early morning or late afternoon for stunning light and fewer people.

Pass/Permit/Fees: Free to visit.

Did You Know? The name Pololu means long spear in Hawaiian, referring to the valley's shape and depth.

Website: http://noahlangphotography.com/blog/pololu-trail-big-island-hawaii

Saddle Road

Journey through the heart of the Big Island on Saddle Road, a high-altitude highway that cuts between Mauna Kea and Mauna Loa. This road offers travelers an unparalleled look at Hawaii's diverse landscapes, from lush rainforests to barren volcanic deserts. Along the way, you can enjoy stunning viewpoints, rare flora and fauna, and even a potential visit to Mauna Kea's summit, where some of the world's best astronomical observatories are located. Saddle Road provides a dramatic and scenic crossing of the island's volcanic backbone.

Location: PFXF+J9 Waimea, Hawaii

Closest City or Town: Waimea, Hawaii

How to Get There: From Hilo, take Saddle Road (HI-200) westbound; from Kona, take Saddle Road eastbound.

GPS Coordinates: 19.6822689° N, 155.4010204° W

Best Time to Visit: Daytime for clear visibility and safer driving conditions.

Pass/Permit/Fees: Free to drive; various fees may apply for Mauna Kea observatories.

Did You Know? Saddle Road was once considered one of the most dangerous roads in Hawaii due to its treacherous conditions but has since been significantly improved.

Website: https://www.hawaii-guide.com/big-island/regions/saddle-road

KAILUA-KONA

Hulihe'e Palace

Step into history at Hulihe'e Palace, a former royal vacation home located in Kailua-Kona on the Big Island. This beautifully preserved palace offers a glimpse into Hawaii's royal past with its period furnishings and artifacts. Situated along Ali'i Drive, visitors can explore the palace's grand rooms and lush gardens while learning about the monarchs who once resided here. Hulihe'e Palace is a cultural gem that transports visitors to a bygone era of Hawaiian royalty.

Location: 75-5718 Alii Dr, Kailua-Kona, Island of Hawaii, HI 96740-1702

Closest City or Town: Kailua-Kona, Hawaii

How to Get There: From Kailua-Kona, head southeast on Queen Ka'ahumanu Highway, turn right onto Palani Road, and follow it to Ali'i Drive.

GPS Coordinates: 19.6393337° N, 155.9943522° W

Best Time to Visit: Year-round, with guided tours available.

Pass/Permit/Fees: Entrance fees apply; see the website for details.

Did You Know? Hulihe'e Palace is one of three royal palaces in Hawaii, showcasing Hawaiian history and heritage.

Website: http://huliheepalace.com/

Manini'owali Beach (Kua Bay)

Discover the beauty and serenity of Manini'owali Beach, also known as Kua Bay, located in Kailua-Kona on the Island of Hawaii. This stunning beach boasts turquoise waters, pristine white sands, and a captivating landscape perfect for swimming, snorkeling, and sunbathing. Visitors can enjoy the softness of the sands underfoot and the breathtaking coastal views, making it an ideal spot for relaxation and scenic photography. The unique charm of Kua Bay lies in its crystal-clear waters and tranquil atmosphere, offering an idyllic escape for beach lovers seeking a slice of paradise.

Location: 72-3055 Kakapa Place, Kailua-Kona, Island of Hawaii, HI 96740

Closest City or Town: Kailua-Kona, Hawaii

How to Get There: From Kailua-Kona, take HI-19 north, turn left onto Kukio Nui Drive, and follow signs to Manini'owali Beach.

GPS Coordinates: 19.8106740° N, 156.0063009° W

Best Time to Visit: Early morning or late afternoon to avoid crowds and enjoy cooler temperatures.

Pass/Permit/Fees: Free to visit.

Did You Know? Manini'owali Beach is part of the Kekaha Kai State Park, known for its diverse marine life and excellent snorkeling conditions.

Website: https://bigislandguide.com/maniniowali-beach-kua-bay

Mauna Kea Summit

Ascend to new heights at the Mauna Kea Summit on the Island of Hawaii. Located just off the Mauna Kea Access Road in Hilo, this summit offers unparalleled stargazing opportunities and breathtaking panoramic views. At an elevation of 13,796 feet, Mauna Kea is home to some of the world's most renowned astronomical observatories. Visitors can explore guided tours or self-drive to witness spectacular sunsets, starlit skies, and the vast, serene landscape.

Location: Island of, Mauna Kea Access Rd, Hilo, HI 96720

Closest City or Town: Hilo, Hawaii

How to Get There: From Hilo, take HI-200 west, turn left onto Saddle Road, and follow the Mauna Kea Access Road to the Visitor Information Station.

GPS Coordinates: 19.8230355° N, 155.4694483° W

Best Time to Visit: Evening for stargazing; daytime for summit views.

Pass/Permit/Fees: Free to visit; observatory tours may have fees.

Did You Know? Mauna Kea means White Mountain in Hawaiian, named for its snow-capped peak during winter months.

Website: https://maunakea.com/

Ocean Rider Seahorse Farm

Dive into the enchanting world of seahorses at Ocean Rider Seahorse Farm, nestled on the Keahole Coast in Kailua-Kona. This unique farm offers visitors a rare opportunity to learn about seahorse conservation through guided tours, interactive exhibits, and up-close encounters. Explore the fascinating marine life, discover the farm's sustainable practices, and even hold a seahorse in your hands. The farm's commitment to ocean conservation and the delicate charm of seahorses make this a magical experience for all ages.

Location: 73-4388 Ilikai Place Keahole Coast, Kailua-Kona, Island of Hawaii, HI 96740

Closest City or Town: Kailua-Kona, Hawaii

How to Get There: From Kailua-Kona, drive north on HI-19, turn left onto Kaiminani Drive, then take a right onto Ilikai Place.

GPS Coordinates: 19.7231317° N, 156.0565020° W

Best Time to Visit: Morning for guided tours and active marine life.

Pass/Permit/Fees: Tour fees apply; visit the website for details.

Did You Know? Ocean Rider Seahorse Farm is the first and only seahorse aquaculture facility in the United States.

Website: http://www.seahorse.com/

The Vanillerie

Explore the fragrant beauty of The Vanillerie, a charming vanilla farm located in Kailua-Kona on the Island of Hawaii. This lush farm offers guided tours where visitors can learn about the intricate process of growing and curing vanilla beans. Wander through the verdant orchards, savor the sweet aroma of vanilla, and sample delicious vanilla-flavored treats. The Vanillerie's dedication to sustainable farming and its picturesque setting create an enchanting and educational experience.

Location: 73-4301 Laui St, Kailua-Kona, Island of Hawaii, HI 96740-9010

Closest City or Town: Kailua-Kona, Hawaii

How to Get There: From Kailua-Kona, take HI-19 north, turn right onto Hina Lani Street, then turn left onto Laui Street.

GPS Coordinates: 19.7267957° N, 156.0257654° W

Best Time to Visit: Morning to early afternoon for tours and tastings.

Pass/Permit/Fees: Tour fees apply; check the website for details.

Did You Know? The Vanillerie is one of the few places in the world where you can witness the complete vanilla cultivation process from flower to pod.

Website: http://www.thevanillerie.com/

NAALEHU

Papakolea Green Sand Beach

Embark on a trek to the unique Papakolea Green Sand Beach, located near South Point on the Big Island of Hawaii. This rare destination, one of only four green sand beaches in the world, owes its distinctive color to the presence of the mineral olivine. Accessing this hidden gem requires a 2.5-mile hike across rugged terrain, but the reward is a secluded, emerald-hued beach enclosed by steep cliffs. A visit here promises an unforgettable experience blending adventure, geology, and natural beauty.

Location: W9P3+C6 Naalehu, Hawaii

Closest City or Town: Naalehu, Hawaii

How to Get There: From Naalehu, drive south on South Point Road until the parking area, then hike approximately 2.5 miles to reach the beach.

GPS Coordinates: 18.9360625° N, 155.6469375° W

Best Time to Visit: Morning to early afternoon for optimal light and manageable temperatures.

Pass/Permit/Fees: Free to visit.

Did You Know? The green sand at Papakolea Beach is formed from olivine crystals found in the surrounding volcanic rocks.

Website: https://bigislandhikes.com/papakolea-green-sand-beach

PAAUILO

Hawaiian Vanilla Company

Indulge in the rich flavors of Hawaiian Vanilla Company, a unique farm located in Paauilo on the Island of Hawaii. Here, visitors can tour the lush vanilla orchards, learn about the cultivation and curing process, and savor vanilla-infused dishes at the on-site café. Participate in tasting experiences and workshops that highlight the versatile uses of vanilla. Nestled in the scenic hills, it's a delightful destination offering both culinary and educational experiences. The farm's dedication to artisanal production makes it a sweet spot for food enthusiasts.

Location: 43-2007 Paauilo Mauka Rd, Paauilo, Island of Hawaii, HI 96776

Closest City or Town: Paauilo, Hawaii

How to Get There: From Hilo, take Saddle Road (HI-200) west, turn right onto Mana Road, then follow signs to Paauilo and the farm.

GPS Coordinates: 20.0284015° N, 155.4095639° W

Best Time to Visit: Morning to early afternoon for tours and tastings.

Pass/Permit/Fees: Tour fees apply; check the website for details.

Did You Know? Hawaiian Vanilla Company was the first commercially grown vanilla operation in the United States.

Website: http://www.hawaiianvanilla.com/

PAHALA

Punalu'u Black Sand Beach

Feel the unique texture of volcanic origin at Punalu'u Black Sand Beach, located along Ninole Loop Road in Pahala on the Island of Hawaii. This beach is famous for its jet-black sand and its frequent visitors—Hawaiian green sea turtles basking under the sun. Visitors can swim, snorkel, or simply walk along the striking black shoreline while marveling at the natural beauty. The beach's distinct sand and the chance to spot sea turtles make Punalu'u a captivating destination for nature lovers.

Location: Ninole Loop Rd, Pahala, Island of Hawaii, HI 96777

Closest City or Town: Pahala, Hawaii

How to Get There: From Pahala, take HI-11 South, then turn onto Ninole Loop Road and follow signs to the beach.

GPS Coordinates: 19.1360065° N, 155.5048603° W

Best Time to Visit: Morning or late afternoon for cooler temperatures and fewer crowds.

Pass/Permit/Fees: Free to visit

Did You Know? Punalu'u means "spring diver" in Hawaiian, hinting at the freshwater springs that mix with the ocean water.

Website: https://www.gohawaii.com/islands/hawaii-big-island/regions/kau/punaluu-black-sand-beach

Papaikou

Hawaii Tropical Botanical Garden

Immerse yourself in the lush biodiversity of Hawaii Tropical Botanical Garden, nestled on the scenic Hamakua Coast of the Island of Hawaii. This verdant paradise features over 2,000 species of tropical plants, flowing waterfalls, and scenic ocean views. Visitors can wander along the meandering paths, marvel at exotic blooms, and enjoy guided tours to learn about the garden's conservation efforts. The garden's vibrant plant life and tranquil ambiance make it a haven for botany enthusiasts and nature lovers alike.

Location: 27-717 Old Mamalahoa Hwy, Papaikou, Island of Hawaii, HI 96781-7746

Closest City or Town: Papaikou, Hawaii

How to Get There: From Hilo, take HI-19 north, turn right onto Old Mamalahoa Highway, and follow signs to the botanical garden.

GPS Coordinates: 19.8109300° N, 155.0960955° W

Best Time to Visit: Morning to enjoy the garden at its freshest and most vibrant

Pass/Permit/Fees: Admission fees apply; see the website for details

Did You Know? The garden was founded by Dan J. Lutkenhouse, who dedicated nearly a decade to transforming a neglected valley into this tropical sanctuary.

Website: http://www.htbg.com/

PUAKO

Hapuna Beach State Recreation Area

Discover paradise at Hapuna Beach State Recreation Area, a pristine oasis located in Puako on the Island of Hawaii. This stunning white-sand beach invites visitors to bask in the sun, swim in the clear, blue waters, and enjoy excellent snorkeling and bodyboarding. With its picturesque setting and vibrant marine life, it's perfect for a day of relaxation or adventure. The park also offers picnic areas and trails for exploring the natural beauty. Known as one of Hawaii's best beaches, Hapuna Beach provides an unforgettable coastal escape.

Location: Old Puako Rd, Puako, Island of Hawaii, HI 96743

Closest City or Town: Puako, Hawaii

How to Get There: From Kailua-Kona, take Queen Kaahumanu Hwy (HI-19) north, turn left onto Hapuna Beach Road, and follow the signs to the park.

GPS Coordinates: 19.9913889° N, 155.8250000° W

Best Time to Visit: Morning for calm waters and fewer crowds.

Pass/Permit/Fees: Free to visit, parking fees may apply.

Did You Know? Hapuna Beach is often ranked among the top beaches in the world for its spectacular beauty and amenities.

Website: http://dlnr.hawaii.gov/dsp/parks/hawaii/hapuna-beach-state-recreation-area/

KAUAI

HANALEI

Hanalei Beach

Unveil the magic of Hanalei Beach, a serene stretch of sand nestled in Hanalei, Kauai. Known for its crescent-shaped bay and majestic mountain backdrop, this beach offers tranquil swimming, paddleboarding, and surfing in its gentle waves. Located on the island's north shore, visitors can stroll along the beach, explore the historic Hanalei Pier, or simply relax under swaying palm trees. Hanalei Beach is unique for its pristine beauty, making it a perfect destination for families, couples, and solo travelers seeking peace and natural splendor. Engage in local culture and enjoy the welcoming aloha spirit that permeates this stunning locale.

Location: 6F2V+XQ Hanalei, Hawaii

Closest City or Town: Hanalei, Kauai, HI

How to Get There: From Lihue, take HI-56 N to HI-560 W and follow signs to Hanalei Beach.

GPS Coordinates: 22.2028472° N, 159.5046669° W

Best Time to Visit: Summer for calm waters; winter for surfing.

Pass/Permit/Fees: Free to visit.

Did You Know? Hanalei means lei-making or crescent bay in Hawaiian, perfectly describing its stunning shape and charm.

Website: https://www.parrishkauai.com/6266/hanalei-bay-kauai-beaches/

KAPAA

Kauai's Hindu Monastery

Experience the spiritual serenity of Kauai's Hindu Monastery, an exquisite sanctuary on the lush island of Kauai. Visitors are welcomed to explore the temple grounds, meditate in tranquil gardens, and marvel at the intricate stonework of the Iraivan Temple. This sacred site offers a unique glimpse into Hindu culture and spirituality, providing a peaceful retreat amid the island's natural beauty.

Location: 107 Kaholalele Rd, Kapaa, Kauai, HI 96746-9304

Closest City or Town: Kapaa, Kauai

How to Get There: From Lihue, take HI-580 N, turn right onto Kaholalele Road, and follow signs to the monastery.

GPS Coordinates: 22.0577410° N, 159.3928800° W

Best Time to Visit: Morning to early afternoon for guided walks and meditation.

Pass/Permit/Fees: Free to visit; donations are appreciated.

Did You Know? The Iraivan Temple is constructed entirely of white granite hand-carved in India.

Website: http://www.himalayanacademy.com/

Lydgate Farms Kauai Chocolate

Savor the sweet delight of Lydgate Farms Kauai Chocolate, a family-run farm located in Kapaa, Kauai. Enjoy guided tours through cacao orchards, learn about the chocolate-making process, and indulge in tastings of award-winning Hawaiian chocolate. This farm offers a delightful experience for food lovers and those interested in sustainable agriculture, providing a behind-the-scenes look at artisanal chocolate production.

Location: 5730 Olohena Rd, Kapaa, Kauai, HI 96746-8808

Closest City or Town: Kapaa, Kauai

How to Get There: From Lihue, take HI-56 N, turn right onto Kawaihau Road, then left on Olohena Road to reach the farm.

GPS Coordinates: 22.0792437° N, 159.3596406° W

Best Time to Visit: Morning for cooler temperatures and scheduled tours.

Pass/Permit/Fees: Tour fees apply; visit their website for details.

Did You Know? Lydgate Farms is home to some of the rarest cacao varieties in the world.

Website: https://lydgatefarms.com/

Sleeping Giant Trail

Embark on an invigorating adventure on the Sleeping Giant Trail, also known as Nounou Mountain Trail, located in Kapaa, Kauai. This moderate hike offers stunning panoramic views of the island and the Pacific Ocean. Climb through lush forests and up steep slopes to reach the mountain's summit, where the giant appears to be resting. It's a perfect trail for nature lovers and photographers looking to capture Kauai's natural beauty from above.

Location: Haleilio Road, Kapaa, Kauai, HI 96746

Closest City or Town: Kapaa, Kauai

How to Get There: From Kapaa, follow Haleilio Road to the trailhead at the end of the road.

GPS Coordinates: 22.0613558° N, 159.3466352° W

Best Time to Visit: Early morning for cooler temperatures and clear views.

Pass/Permit/Fees: Free to hike.

Did You Know? The trail is part of the Nounou Mountain range, which locals say resembles a sleeping giant.

Website: https://www.alltrails.com/trail/hawaii/kaua-i--2/sleeping-giant-nounou-mountain-east-trail

KAUAI

Hanalei Bay

Discover the breathtaking beauty of Hanalei Bay, a stunning spot nestled in Hanalei, Kauai. Known for its picturesque crescent-shaped bay and lush green mountains, this beach offers a tranquil retreat with opportunities for surfing, paddleboarding, and swimming. Walk along the historic Hanalei Pier or relax on the soft sandy shores. Hanalei Bay is perfect for families, couples, and solo travelers longing for a peaceful beach experience.

Location: 6F2V+XQ Hanalei, Hawaii

Closest City or Town: Hanalei, Hawaii

How to Get There: From Lihue, take HI-56 N to HI-560 W and follow signs to Hanalei Bay.

GPS Coordinates: 22.2090776° N, 159.5067583° W

Best Time to Visit: Summer for calm waters; winter for surfing.

Pass/Permit/Fees: Free to visit.

Did You Know? Hanalei Bay's name means lei-making or crescent bay in Hawaiian, aptly describing its shape and charm.

Website: https://www.gohawaii.com/islands/kauai

Kalalau Lookout

Be mesmerized by the panoramic views at Kalalau Lookout, one of Kauai's most breathtaking viewpoints. Located along Kokee Road, this lookout offers stunning vistas of the Kalalau Valley and the dramatic Na Pali Coast. On a clear day, you can see the vibrant greens of the valley juxtaposed against the deep blues of the Pacific Ocean. This spot is perfect for photography, meditation, and appreciating the grandeur of Kauai's untouched beauty.

Location: Kokee Rd Kapa'a, Kauai, HI 96746

Closest City or Town: Kapa'a, Hawaii

How to Get There: From Waimea, take HI-550 north (Kokee Road) and follow signs to Kalalau Lookout.

GPS Coordinates: 22.1511297° N, 159.6459593° W

Best Time to Visit: Early morning or late afternoon for the best light and fewer clouds.

Pass/Permit/Fees: Free to visit.

Did You Know? Kalalau Lookout sits at an elevation of 4,000 feet, offering one of the highest accessible views of the island.

Website: http://liveinhawaiinow.com/kalalau-lookout/

Kalalau Trail

Embrace the spirit of adventure on the Kalalau Trail, a world-renowned hiking route located on Kauai's Na Pali Coast. Spanning 11 miles, this trail offers spectacular views, challenging terrain, and lush landscapes. Hike through verdant valleys, past soaring cliffs, and along pristine beaches. The trail's ultimate reward is reaching the secluded Kalalau Beach, a paradise at the end of an epic journey.

Location: 59RH+CW Kapaa, Hawaii

Closest City or Town: Kapaa, Hawaii

How to Get There: From Hanalei, drive west on Kuhio Highway until you reach the trailhead at Ha'ena State Park.

GPS Coordinates: 22.1958872° N, 159.6203563° W

Best Time to Visit: Dry season (May to October) for safer hiking conditions.

Pass/Permit/Fees: Permit required for overnight camping; entry fees apply for Ha'ena State Park.

Did You Know? The Kalalau Trail is the only land access to the Na Pali Coast, offering a unique glimpse into one of Hawaii's most remote areas.

Website: https://kalalautrail.com/

Tunnels Beach

Find your sense of wonder at Tunnels Beach, a breathtaking destination located in Hanalei, Kauai. This well-known beach offers visitors a unique underwater world, boasting some of the best snorkeling and diving opportunities in Hawaii. Encounter vibrant coral reefs, marine life, and crystal-clear waters, all backed by the stunning cliffs of Kauai's north shore. A scenic spot for beach activities, Tunnels Beach is also perfect for sunbathing and picnicking, providing a memorable seaside escape.

Location: 5-6607 Kuhio Hwy, Hanalei, Kauai, HI 96714

Closest City or Town: Hanalei, Kauai

How to Get There: From Hanalei, take the Kuhio Highway westbound for about 8 miles until you reach the beach parking area.

GPS Coordinates: 22.2229479° N, 159.5522669° W

Best Time to Visit: Summer months for calm seas and optimal snorkeling conditions.

Pass/Permit/Fees: Free to visit.

Did You Know? Tunnels Beach was the filming location for the 1958 film South Pacific.

Website: https://www.kauai.com/tunnels-beach

KILAUEA

Garden Island Chocolate

Indulge in a delicious adventure at Garden Island Chocolate, a charming farm located in Kilauea, Kauai. Immerse yourself in the world of artisan chocolate with guided tours that take you through the cacao orchards, teaching you about the chocolate-making process from bean to bar. Savor samples of exquisite homemade chocolate, explore the lush, tropical farm, and enjoy the sweet aroma of cacao. This farm offers a sensory and educational experience, making it a must-visit for chocolate lovers.

Location: 6020 Koolaur Road, Kilauea, Kauai, HI 96754-5143

Closest City or Town: Kilauea, Kauai

How to Get There: From Kilauea, head west on Kuhio Highway, turn right on Kalihiwai Road, follow the signs to the farm.

GPS Coordinates: 22.1780593° N, 159.3245725° W

Best Time to Visit: Morning tours offer cooler temperatures and a more immersive experience.

Pass/Permit/Fees: Tour fees apply; see the website for details.

Did You Know? Garden Island Chocolate uses sustainable farming practices to produce some of the finest chocolates in Hawaii.

Website: http://www.gardenislandchocolate.com/

Hawaiian Organic Noni

Explore the health benefits of noni at Hawaiian Organic Noni, an organic farm located in Kilauea, Kauai. Learn about the cultivation and processing of the noni fruit, known for its medicinal properties, through informative tours. Embrace the opportunity to taste fresh noni products and discover their various health benefits. With its focus on sustainable farming and natural wellbeing, this farm provides a unique and insightful experience.

Location: 11 Larson Beach Rd, Kilauea, Kauai, HI 96754

Closest City or Town: Kilauea, Kauai

How to Get There: From Kilauea, take Kuhio Highway to Kalihiwai Road, continue onto Larson Beach Road until you reach the farm.

GPS Coordinates: 22.1974132° N, 159.3423083° W

Best Time to Visit: Morning for guided tours and tastings.

Pass/Permit/Fees: Tour fees apply; visit the website for details.

Did You Know? Noni juice is traditionally used in Polynesian medicine for its anti-inflammatory and immune-boosting properties.

Website: http://realnoni.com/Noni-Farm-Tour/

LIHUE

Kauai Museum

Delve into the rich tapestry of Kauai's history at the Kauai Museum in Lihue. This hidden gem provides an insightful journey through the island's heritage, from the ancient Hawaiian artifacts to the plantation era and beyond. Located near the historic Wilcox Building, the museum is a treasure trove of cultural relics and riveting exhibits. Visitors can attend diverse events, enjoy educational programs, and explore two galleries filled with enchanting stories of Kauai's past.

Location: 4428 Rice Street, Lihue, Kauai, HI 96766-1338

Closest City or Town: Lihue, Kauai

How to Get There: From Lihue Airport, head southwest on Ahukini Rd, then turn right on Kuhio Hwy. Turn left on Rice Street; the museum is on the right.

GPS Coordinates: 21.9750350° N, 159.3682530° W

Best Time to Visit: Weekday mornings for a quieter experience.

Pass/Permit/Fees: Admission fees apply; check the website for details.

Did You Know? The Kauai Museum's building was originally constructed as a library in 1924.

Website: http://www.kauaimuseum.org/

Kilohana Plantation

Unearth the allure of a bygone era at Kilohana Plantation in Lihue, Kauai. Spanning 104 lush acres, this former sugar plantation offers activities like train tours, rum tasting, and a visit to the on-site shops and restaurants. The estate's grand mansion, dating back to the 1930s, is a charming relic of the island's plantation heritage. Explore tropical gardens, marvel at historic architecture, and relish local flavors at Gaylord's Restaurant within the estate.

Location: 3-2087 Kaumualii Hwy, Lihue, Kauai, HI 96766-9505

Closest City or Town: Lihue, Kauai

How to Get There: From Lihue Airport, take Ahukini Rd, then turn right on Kuhio Hwy south. Merge onto HI-50 and the plantation is on the left.

GPS Coordinates: 21.9714003° N, 159.3914129° W

Best Time to Visit: Late morning to early afternoon for tours and dining.

Pass/Permit/Fees: Entry is free, fees apply for specific tours and activities.

Did You Know? Kilohana Plantation was once the most productive sugar plantation in Kauai.

Website: http://www.kilohanakauai.com/

Wailua Falls

Marvel at the sheer beauty of Wailua Falls, a spectacular double waterfall located just outside Lihue, Kauai. This stunning natural wonder plummets 80 feet into a pool below, often creating rainbows in the mist. Easily accessible by car, visitors can enjoy the breathtaking views and capture beautiful photographs from the viewing area above the falls.

Location: 3610 Rice St Marriott Resort, Lihue, Kauai, HI 96766-1705

Closest City or Town: Lihue, Kauai

How to Get There: From Lihue, drive northeast on Maalo Rd (HI-583) until you reach the falls.

GPS Coordinates: 21.9620979° N, 159.3499131° W

Best Time to Visit: Early morning for serene views and fewer crowds.

Pass/Permit/Fees: Free to visit

Did You Know? Wailua Falls are featured in the opening credits of the television show Fantasy Island.

Website:
https://www.gohawaii.com/islands/kauai/regions/lihue/wailua-falls

POIPU

Poipu Beach Park

Take in the sun and surf at Poipu Beach Park, a picturesque seaside destination in Poipu, Koloa, Kauai. Known for its golden sands and tranquil waters, it's a perfect spot for swimming, snorkeling, and family fun. Watch for Hawaiian monk seals basking on the shore or enjoy a picnic under swaying palm trees. This park's unique charm lies in its dual bays, making it a versatile haven for water sports enthusiasts and sunbathers alike.

Location: 2179 Hoone Road, Poipu, Koloa, Kauai, HI 96756

Closest City or Town: Koloa, Hawaii

How to Get There: From Lihue, take HI-50 West, turn left on Maluhia Road, follow signs to Poipu Road, and turn right onto Hoone Road.

GPS Coordinates: 21.8736270° N, 159.4547973° W

Best Time to Visit: Early morning for calm seas and fewer crowds.

Pass/Permit/Fees: Free to visit.

Did You Know? Poipu Beach was named one of America's best beaches by the Travel Channel.

Website: https://www.gohawaii.com/islands/kauai/regions/south-shore/poipu-beach-park

Spouting Horn

Witness the awe-inspiring natural phenomenon of Spouting Horn, a dramatic blowhole located near Koloa on the south shore of Kauai. As waves crash into a lava tube, water is forced upward, creating a spectacular spout that sometimes shoots as high as 50 feet into the air. The accompanying hiss and roar add to the allure of this seaside marvel, making it a must-see attraction for nature lovers and photographers.

Location: VGP4+5F Koloa, Hawaii, Stati Uniti

Closest City or Town: Koloa, Hawaii

How to Get There: From Poipu, drive west on Lawai Road until you reach the designated parking area for Spouting Horn.

GPS Coordinates: 21.8854375° N, 159.4938125° W

Best Time to Visit: Late afternoon for impressive spouts against a scenic sunset.

Pass/Permit/Fees: Free to visit.

Did You Know? The name "Spouting Horn" comes from the loud sound that resembles a dragon's roar when water shoots through the blowhole.

Website: https://www.gohawaii.com/islands/kauai/regions/south-shore/spouting-horn

PRINCEVILLE

Hanalei Valley Lookout

Soak in the breathtaking panorama at Hanalei Valley Lookout, nestled along Kuhio Highway in Princeville, Kauai. This scenic viewpoint offers sweeping views of lush taro fields, verdant mountains, and the meandering Hanalei River. Ideal for sunrise or sunset, the lookout provides a perfect spot for photography and contemplation, showcasing the natural beauty that defines Kauai's north shore.

Location: Kuhio Hwy, Princeville, Kauai, HI 96722

Closest City or Town: Princeville, Hawaii

How to Get There: From Lihue, take HI-56 North past Hanalei Bridge to the marked lookout on the left side of the highway.

GPS Coordinates: 22.2127190° N, 159.4756572° W

Best Time to Visit: Early morning or late afternoon for optimal lighting.

Pass/Permit/Fees: Free to visit.

Did You Know? The Hanalei Valley is one of the most fertile farming areas in Hawaii, producing most of the state's taro.

Website:
https://www.facebook.com/profile.php?id=425904660781705

Princeville Botanical Gardens

Enter a tropical paradise at Princeville Botanical Gardens in Princeville, Kauai. These family-owned gardens offer guided tours through their lush landscapes filled with exotic flowers, rare and endangered plants, and diverse fruit trees. Learn about traditional Hawaiian medicinal plants and immerse yourself in vibrant surroundings, making it a perfect retreat for nature enthusiasts and horticultural aficionados.

Location: 3840 Ahonui Pl, Princeville, Kauai, HI 96722-5530

Closest City or Town: Princeville, Hawaii

How to Get There: From Lihue, travel north on HI-56, turn right on Ka Haku Road, and follow the signs to the gardens.

GPS Coordinates: 22.1973754° N, 159.4536946° W

Best Time to Visit: Morning tours for cooler conditions and active guide sessions.

Pass/Permit/Fees: Tour fees apply; visit the website for details.

Did You Know? The gardens feature cacao trees and offer chocolate tastings as part of the tour experience.

Website: https://kauaibotanicalgardens.com/

Queen's Bath

Explore the natural wonder of Queen's Bath, a serene tide pool situated in Princeville, Kauai. This unique spot offers an unforgettable swimming experience amidst volcanic rock formations with stunning ocean views. Accessible via a short hike, Queen's Bath is a hidden gem where visitors can bask in calm waters or marvel at the surrounding marine life in crystal-clear pools.

Location: Kapiolani Loop, Princeville, Kauai, HI 96722

Closest City or Town: Princeville, Hawaii

How to Get There: From Princeville, drive north along Ka Haku Road, turn left onto Punahele Road, and follow signs to the trailhead.

GPS Coordinates: 22.2292315° N, 159.4874367° W

Best Time to Visit: Summer months for safer swimming conditions.

Pass/Permit/Fees: Free to visit.

Did You Know? Queen's Bath was named for its past use as a royal bathing place for Hawaiian chiefs.

Website: https://en.wikipedia.org/wiki/Queen%27s_Bath

WAIMEA

Waimea Canyon State Park

Discover the Grand Canyon of the Pacific at Waimea Canyon State Park in Kauai. This immense, colorful canyon offers stunning vistas, rugged terrain, and deep gorges. Take a scenic drive along Waimea Canyon Drive to numerous lookout points, hike through forested trails, and admire cascading waterfalls. Whether you're adventuring on foot or enjoying a picnic with a view, this natural wonder is a must-visit for its awe-inspiring landscapes and panoramic views.

Location: Waimea Canyon Dr, Waimea, Kauai, HI 96796

Closest City or Town: Waimea, Kauai

How to Get There: From Waimea town, head north on HI-550 (Waimea Canyon Drive); the park is clearly signposted along the road.

GPS Coordinates: 22.0726785° N, 159.6656013° W

Best Time to Visit: Late morning to early afternoon when visibility is at its best.

Pass/Permit/Fees: Entry fees may apply; check the website for details.

Did You Know? Waimea Canyon spans approximately 14 miles long, 1 mile wide, and over 3,600 feet deep.

Website: https://dlnr.hawaii.gov/dsp/parks/kauai/waimea-canyon-state-park/

Nā Pali Coast State Park

Find yourself amidst the dramatic landscapes of Nā Pali Coast State Park, located on Kauai's northern shore. Famous for its emerald cliffs, sea caves, and waterfalls, this park is a haven for adventurous souls. Hike the renowned Kalalau Trail, embark on a boat tour, or view the rugged coast from a helicopter. The park's unparalleled beauty and remote wilderness offer an experience like no other, making it a quintessential Hawaiian adventure.

Location: 5-8291 Kuhio Hwy, Hanalei, Kauai, HI 96714

Closest City or Town: Hanalei, Kauai

How to Get There: From Hanalei, take Kuhio Highway north until you reach Ha'ena State Park, the gateway to the Nā Pali Coast.

GPS Coordinates: 22.2219152° N, 159.5454656° W

Best Time to Visit: Dry season (May to October) for safer hiking and boat tours.

Pass/Permit/Fees: Permit required for overnight camping; day-use entry is free.

Did You Know? Nā Pali means high cliffs in Hawaiian, perfectly describing its steep and breathtaking coastal terrain.

Website: https://www.hawaiistateparks.org/parks/napali-coast-state-wilderness-park/

LANAI

LANAI CITY

Mike Carroll Gallery

Step into a world oozing with artistic charm at Mike Carroll Gallery, nestled in the heart of Lanai City, Lanai. This enchanting gallery showcases vibrant works of art, from local landscapes to Hawaiian culture captured vividly on canvas. Opened by former Chicago artist Mike Carroll, the gallery offers a welcoming space to enjoy and purchase original pieces. Visitors can lose themselves exploring the artwork, attend artist receptions, and even meet Mike Carroll himself.

Location: 443 7th St., Lanai City, Lanai, HI 96763

Closest City or Town: Lanai City, Lanai

How to Get There: From Lanai Airport, drive south on Kaumalapau Hwy, turn right on 7th St., and the gallery will be on your left.

GPS Coordinates: 20.8263570° N, 156.9194667° W

Best Time to Visit: Mid-morning to early afternoon when the gallery is most active.

Pass/Permit/Fees: Free entry

Did You Know? Mike Carroll was originally a political cartoonist before moving to Lanai and opening his gallery.

Website: http://www.mikecarrollgallery.com/

MAUI

KULA

Haleakala Crater

Discover the otherworldly landscapes of Haleakala Crater, located along Haleakala Highway in Kula, Maui. Rising over 10,000 feet above sea level, this dormant volcano offers breathtaking views of the expansive crater and its unique geological formations. Visitors can hike along the various trails, witness the sunrise from the summit, or explore the diverse flora and fauna that thrive in this high-altitude environment. The surreal beauty of Haleakala Crater makes it a must-see destination for nature lovers and adventure seekers alike.

Location: Haleakala Hwy, Kula, Maui, HI 96790

Closest City or Town: Kula, Maui

How to Get There: From Kahului, take HI-37 and then Haleakala Highway 378 to the summit.

GPS Coordinates: 20.7137645° N, 156.2498190° W

Best Time to Visit: Sunrise for magnificent views and fewer clouds.

Pass/Permit/Fees: Entrance fee to Haleakala National Park applies.

Did You Know? Haleakala means House of the Sun in Hawaiian, reflecting its significance in local mythology.

Website: http://www.nps.gov/hale/index.htm

Haleakala National Park

Discover the otherworldly landscapes of Haleakala National Park, an awe-inspiring site located in Kula, Maui. Ascend over 10,000 feet above sea level to witness the expansive crater and its unique geological formations. Enjoy hiking along the various trails, marvel at the sunrise from the summit, and explore the diverse flora and fauna that thrive in this high-altitude environment. This national park provides an unforgettable journey through volcanic landscapes and vibrant ecosystems.

Location: PRCV+5W Kula, Hawaii

Closest City or Town: Kula, Maui

How to Get There: From Kahului, take HI-37 and Haleakala Highway 378 to the park entrance.

GPS Coordinates: 20.7203826° N, 156.1551524° W

Best Time to Visit: Sunrise for magnificent views and fewer clouds.

Pass/Permit/Fees: Entrance fee to Haleakala National Park applies.

Did You Know? Haleakala means House of the Sun in Hawaiian, reflecting its significance in local mythology.

Website: http://www.nps.gov/hale/index.htm

O'o Farm

Step into the heart of Maui's upcountry with a visit to O'o Farm, located in Kula. Discover the magic of farm-to-table dining as you stroll through the lush fields where fresh produce is cultivated. Participate in a hands-on farm tour that culminates in a gourmet lunch prepared with ingredients harvested from the grounds. The serene setting offers a perfect escape and a chance to reconnect with nature. Unique in its dedication to sustainable farming practices, O'o Farm promises a delightful culinary adventure in an idyllic landscape.

Location: 651 Waipoli Rd, Kula, Maui, HI 96790-7822

Closest City or Town: Kula, Maui

How to Get There: From Kahului, take HI-37 to Omaopio Road, follow it uphill to Waipoli Road, and continue to the farm.

GPS Coordinates: 20.7370660° N, 156.3233246° W

Best Time to Visit: Morning tours offer the freshest experience.

Pass/Permit/Fees: Tour fees apply; see the website for current rates.

Did You Know? O'o Farm sits on eight acres and grows a remarkable variety of organic produce used in local Maui restaurants.

Website: http://www.oofarm.com/default.htm

Pipiwai Trail

Lose yourself in the tropical beauty of the Pipiwai Trail, located at Mile Marker 41 on Hana Highway, within Haleakala National Park on Maui. This 4-mile round-trip trail meanders through lush bamboo forests and past stunning waterfalls, culminating at the breathtaking Waimoku Falls. Hikers can enjoy crossing picturesque footbridges and taking in the exotic flora and fauna that adorn this idyllic path. The Pipiwai Trail provides a sanctuary for nature enthusiasts, offering an unforgettable journey through one of Hawaii's most beautiful landscapes.

Location: Mile Marker 41 Hana Hwy, Haleakala National Park, Maui, HI 96713

Closest City or Town: Hana, Maui

How to Get There: From Hana, drive west on Hana Highway to Mile Marker 41 and follow signs to the Pipiwai Trailhead.

GPS Coordinates: 20.7203826° N, 156.1551524° W

Best Time to Visit: Early morning to avoid crowds and afternoon heat.

Pass/Permit/Fees: Entrance fee to Haleakala National Park applies.

Did You Know? The Pipiwai Trail leads to Waimoku Falls, which cascades down 400 feet into a serene pool.

Website: https://www.nps.gov/hale/planyourvisit/kipahulu.htm

Surfing Goat Dairy

Find your sense of fun at Surfing Goat Dairy, a delightful farm located in Kula, Maui. Engage in interactive tours where you can milk a goat, taste award-winning cheeses, and learn about sustainable dairy farming. This spread of green pastureland not only offers a peek into the happy lives of its resident goats but also invites you to savor the fine culinary products crafted from their milk. Kids and adults alike will love the playful ambiance and hands-on experiences unique to this charming dairy farm.

HAWAII BUCKET LIST

Location: 3651 Omaopio Rd, Kula, Maui, HI 96790-8871

Closest City or Town: Kula, Maui

How to Get There: From Kahului, drive south on HI-37, turn left onto Omaopio Road, and continue until you see the signs for Surfing Goat Dairy.

GPS Coordinates: 20.8066645° N, 156.3651570° W

Best Time to Visit: Morning for the milking tours.

Pass/Permit/Fees: Tour fees apply; visit the website for details.

Did You Know? Surfing Goat Dairy's cheeses have won more than 18 national awards, making it a must-visit for cheese lovers.

Website: http://www.surfinggoatdairy.com/

HANA

Wai'anapanapa State Park

Dive into the breathtaking beauty of Wai'anapanapa State Park, a coastal gem located near Hana, Maui. This park offers a stunning black sand beach, freshwater caves, sea arches, and dramatic lava cliffs, making it a paradise for adventurers and nature lovers. Located along the Hana Highway, visitors can explore tide pools, hike the coastal trails, and even glimpse the legendary fresh water caves. The park is unique for its rich cultural history, including ancient Hawaiian burial sites and historical trails. A visit to Wai'anapanapa promises an awe-inspiring experience amidst the wild landscapes of Maui.

Location: Hana Hwy. Near mile marker 32, Hana, Maui, HI 96713

Closest City or Town: Hana, Maui, HI

How to Get There: From Kahului, take the Hana Highway (HI-360 E) towards Hana, near mile marker 32.

GPS Coordinates: 20.8546661° N, 156.1694682° W

Best Time to Visit: Year-round, but spring and fall offer mild weather and fewer crowds.

Pass/Permit/Fees: Park entrance fee: $5 for non-residents.

Did You Know? Wai'anapanapa translates to glistening fresh water, referring to the natural pools found in the park's lava tubes.

Website: https://dlnr.hawaii.gov/dsp/parks/maui/waianapanapa-state-park/

KAPALUA

Dragon's Teeth

Marvel at the natural artistry of Dragon's Teeth, an otherworldly rock formation located in Kapalua, Maui. Formed by centuries of erosion, these jagged, wind-swept rocks resemble a dragon's teeth, adding a mythic beauty to the coastline. Explore the rugged terrain, listen to the waves crashing against the rocks, and take in the breathtaking views of the Pacific Ocean. This unique geological wonder offers a peaceful and dramatic setting for photography and nature appreciation.

Location: Makalua-puna Point off Office Road, Kapalua, Maui, HI 96761

Closest City or Town: Kapalua, Maui

How to Get There: From Lahaina, take HI-30 N to Office Road. Park near the end of Office Road and follow the trail to Makaluapuna Point.

GPS Coordinates: 20.9977890° N, 156.6544130° W

Best Time to Visit: Morning to mid-afternoon for the best lighting and to avoid high tides.

Pass/Permit/Fees: Free to visit.

Did You Know? Dragon's Teeth were formed from lava flows that were solidified by strong winds and powerful ocean currents.

Website: http://liveinhawaiinow.com/dragons-teeth/

Kapalua Beach

Find your perfect beach escape at Kapalua Beach, a serene paradise situated in Lahaina, Maui. This crescent-shaped beach is renowned for its golden sands, tranquil waters, and abundant marine life, making it an excellent spot for snorkeling and swimming. Discover the vibrant underwater world inhabited by colorful fish and gentle sea turtles. With its picturesque backdrop of swaying palm trees and rolling waves, Kapalua Beach offers an idyllic setting for sunbathing, picnicking, and leisurely strolls.

Location: 1 Bay Club Pl, Lahaina, HI 96761

Closest City or Town: Lahaina, Hawaii

How to Get There: From Lahaina, take HI-30 north and turn left onto Office Road, then follow signs to Kapalua Beach.

GPS Coordinates: 20.9983577° N, 156.6671755° W

Best Time to Visit: Morning to early afternoon for calm waters and fewer crowds.

Pass/Permit/Fees: Free to visit.

Did You Know? Kapalua Beach was once a retreat for Hawaiian royalty before becoming a beloved destination for visitors.

Website: https://www.gohawaii.com/islands/maui/regions/west-maui/Kapalua

LAHAINA

Ka'anapali Beach

Embrace the splendor of Ka'anapali Beach, a world-renowned stretch of sun-kissed sand in Maui. This beach paradise offers a plethora of activities, from snorkeling at Black Rock to parasailing and jet skiing. The walkable beachfront resorts, golf courses, and the open-air Whalers Village shopping complex provide ample entertainment and dining options. Ka'anapali's turquoise waters and lively atmosphere make it a perfect spot for both relaxation and adventure.

Location: 100 Nohea Kai Dr, Marriott's Maui Ocean Club, Maui, HI 96761-1917

Closest City or Town: Lahaina, Maui

How to Get There: From Lahaina, take HI-30 north and follow signs to Ka'anapali Beach.

GPS Coordinates: 20.9169059° N, 156.6957594° W

Best Time to Visit: Early morning or sunset for fewer crowds and tranquil views.

Pass/Permit/Fees: Free to visit; parking fees may apply at nearby resorts.

Did You Know? Ka'anapali Beach was Hawaii's first planned resort and has been voted America's Best Beach.

Website: https://mauiguidebook.com/beaches/kaanapali-beach/

Lahaina Banyan Court Park

Discover history and nature intertwined at Lahaina Banyan Court Park in Lahaina, Maui. Home to one of the largest banyan trees in the United States, this park is a botanical marvel offering ample shade and picturesque views. The banyan tree, planted in 1873, has spread across an entire city block. Stroll through the park's shaded walkways, explore the nearby historic courthouse, and enjoy community events that frequently fill the air with spirited activity.

Location: 671 Front St, Lahaina, Maui, HI 96761

Closest City or Town: Lahaina, Maui

How to Get There: From HI-30, turn onto Front Street and proceed to the park located near Lahaina Harbor.

GPS Coordinates: 20.8718511° N, 156.6776043° W

Best Time to Visit: Late afternoon for cooler temperatures and more relaxed ambiance.

Pass/Permit/Fees: Free to visit.

Did You Know? The Lahaina Banyan Tree stands over 60 feet high and has 16 major trunks besides the main trunk, spreading over 200 feet in diameter.

Website: https://www.mauicounty.gov/facilities/Facility/Details/125

MAKAWAO

Maui Pineapple Tour

Savor the sweet experience of a Maui Pineapple Tour, located in the hills of Makawao, Maui. This delightful tour invites visitors to explore pineapple fields and learn about the unique growth process of this tropical fruit. Sample fresh pineapples straight from the fields, gain insights on sustainable farming practices, and even take home a pineapple fresh from the harvest.

Location: 883 Haliimaile Rd, Makawao, Maui, HI 96768-9769

Closest City or Town: Makawao, Maui

How to Get There: From Kahului, take HI-37 east, then turn left onto Haliimaile Rd and follow signs to the tour location.

GPS Coordinates: 20.8686752° N, 156.3406219° W

Best Time to Visit: Morning tours for cooler temperatures and a more enjoyable experience.

Pass/Permit/Fees: Tour fees apply; visit the website for details.

Did You Know? This tour is the only pineapple farm tour in the United States, offering a rare and sweet experience.

Website: http://mauipineappletour.com/

MAUI

Hana Highway Road to Hana

Set off on a mesmerizing adventure along the Hana Highway, a scenic drive stretching from Kahului to Hana on Maui's eastern coast. This iconic route, often called the Road to Hana, unveils awe-inspiring landscapes with lush rainforests, cascading waterfalls, and picturesque coastal views. Wind through 64 miles of hairpin turns and narrow bridges, stopping to explore hidden gems like the Twin Falls, Wailua Falls, and the black sand beach at Waianapanapa State Park. The journey promises not just stunning vistas but also an immersion into the island's natural and cultural richness.

Location: 2910 Hana Hwy, Hana, HI 96713

Closest City or Town: Hana, Hawaii

How to Get There: Starting in Kahului, take HI-36 east, which becomes HI-360. Follow the winding road all the way to Hana.

GPS Coordinates: 20.7820566° N, 156.0203038° W

Best Time to Visit: Early morning to avoid traffic and enjoy a peaceful drive.

Pass/Permit/Fees: Free to drive; some attractions along the way may have entrance fees.

Did You Know? The Hana Highway features over 59 bridges, many of which were built by hand in the early 1900s.

Website: http://www.tourmaui.com/road-to-hana/

PAIA

Ho'okipa Beach Park

Embrace the thrill of the waves at Ho'okipa Beach Park, a world-renowned surf destination located on Maui's north shore. This beach park provides an ideal playground for windsurfing, kite surfing, and traditional surfing, attracting enthusiasts from around the globe. Visitors can watch seasoned surfers tackle the impressive waves or simply relax on the sandy shores while admiring the vibrant sunset. The beach's dynamic ocean conditions and lively atmosphere make Ho'okipa Beach Park a must-visit for ocean lovers and adrenaline junkies.

Location: 179 Hana Hwy, Paia, Maui, HI 96779

Closest City or Town: Paia, Maui

How to Get There: From Paia, take Hana Highway (HI-36) east for about 2 miles. The park entrance will be on the left.

GPS Coordinates: 20.9342545° N, 156.3560790° W

Best Time to Visit: Late afternoon for optimal windsurfing conditions and beautiful sunsets

Pass/Permit/Fees: Free to visit

Did You Know? Ho'okipa Beach is considered one of the premier windsurfing spots in the world.

Website: https://www.mauicounty.gov/facilities/Facility/Details/169

WAILEA

Little Beach

Discover a hidden gem at Little Beach, part of Makena State Park located in Kihei, Maui. Famous for its natural beauty and vibrant sunsets, this secluded spot offers excellent opportunities for sunbathing, swimming, and snorkeling. Embrace the island's free-spirited spirit with its clothing-optional policy and enjoy the lively Sunday evening drum circles. Little Beach, with its turquoise waters and soft sands, provides a serene escape for those seeking an off-the-beaten-path adventure.

Location: JHM3+Q5 Kihei, Hawaii

Closest City or Town: Kihei, Maui

How to Get There: From Kihei, drive south on Makena Alanui Road, follow signs to Makena State Park, and park near Big Beach. Hike over the lava ridge to Little Beach.

GPS Coordinates: 20.6344375° N, 156.4470625° W

Best Time to Visit: Late afternoon for a stunning sunset experience.

Pass/Permit/Fees: Free to visit.

Did You Know? Little Beach is renowned for its Sunday drum circle and fire-dancing performances.

Website: https://www.themauiexpert.com/makena-state-park-little-beach-maui

Wailea Beach

Find your perfect slice of paradise at Wailea Beach, a pristine stretch of sand located in Kihei, Maui. Known for its luxurious surroundings, this beach is ideal for swimming, snorkeling, and sunbathing with its calm, crystal-clear waters. The beachfront is surrounded by upscale resorts, providing easy access to lavish amenities and dining options. Whether it's a leisurely stroll along the golden sands or a rejuvenating dip in the sea, Wailea Beach offers a serene and picturesque Hawaiian getaway.

HAWAII BUCKET LIST

Location: MHM4+4R Kihei, Hawaii

Closest City or Town: Kihei, Maui

How to Get There: From Kihei, drive south on South Kihei Road, continue to Wailea Alanui Drive, and follow signs to Wailea Beach.

GPS Coordinates: 20.6828480° N, 156.4429602° W

Best Time to Visit: Early morning for tranquil waters and fewer crowds.

Pass/Permit/Fees: Free to visit.

Did You Know? Wailea Beach has been consistently ranked among the best beaches in the world.

Website: https://mauiguidebook.com/beaches/wailea-beach/

WAILUKU

Maui Ocean Center

Immerse yourself in the wonders of the sea at Maui Ocean Center, a captivating aquarium located in Wailuku, Maui. This state-of-the-art facility showcases the diverse marine life of the Pacific Ocean through interactive exhibits, a large shark tank, and an enchanting coral reef tunnel. Visitors can marvel at the vibrant array of fish, sea turtles, and rays while learning about marine conservation efforts. Located near Ma'alaea Harbor, it's a family-friendly attraction offering an educational and awe-inspiring experience. The center's immersive displays make it a must-visit.

Location: 192 Ma'alaea Road, Wailuku, Maui, HI 96793-5931

Closest City or Town: Wailuku, Maui

How to Get There: From Kahului, take HI-380 west to HI-30 south, then follow signs to Ma'alaea Harbor and the aquarium.

GPS Coordinates: 20.7926322° N, 156.5121616° W

Best Time to Visit: Morning to mid-afternoon for fewer crowds and active marine life.

Pass/Permit/Fees: Admission fees apply; see the website for details.

Did You Know? The Maui Ocean Center houses one of the largest collections of live coral in the United States.

Website: http://mauioceancenter.com/

Iao Valley State Monument

Immerse yourself in the natural beauty and cultural significance of Iao Valley State Monument, nestled in Wailuku, Maui. This dramatic park is home to the iconic Iao Needle, a lush, green peak rising 1,200 feet from the valley floor. Offering easy-to-navigate trails, the park is perfect for hiking, enjoying the verdant landscape, and exploring the rich history of historic battles fought here. The misty, tropical environment and the imposing Iao Needle make this a captivating destination for nature lovers and history enthusiasts alike.

Location: 54 S High St, Wailuku, Maui, HI 96793-2102

Closest City or Town: Wailuku, Maui

How to Get There: From Kahului, take HI-32 west to Waiehu Beach Rd, then turn onto Iao Valley Rd and follow signs to the park.

GPS Coordinates: 20.8867258° N, 156.5042610° W

Best Time to Visit: Early morning or late afternoon to avoid crowds and enjoy cooler weather.

Pass/Permit/Fees: Entrance fee required; check the website for current rates.

Did You Know? Iao Valley is considered one of the most botanically diverse areas in Hawaii, boasting a wide array of native plants.

Website: https://www.hawaiistateparks.org/parks/iao-valley-state-monument

Maui Tropical Plantation

Immerse yourself in tropical splendor at Maui Tropical Plantation, a lush paradise nestled in the heart of Wailuku, Maui. Experience Hawaii's agricultural heritage firsthand as you explore the vibrant fields, enjoy a tram tour, and sample farm-fresh products. Discover the history and cultivation of sugarcane, pineapples, and coconut, all amidst breathtaking views of the West Maui Mountains. With guided tours, scenic walking paths, and a gourmet restaurant, this plantation offers a perfect blend of education, adventure, and relaxation.

Location: 1670 Honoapiilani Hwy, Wailuku, Maui, HI 96793-9347

Closest City or Town: Wailuku, Maui

How to Get There: From Kahului, take HI-380 to HI-30 W, turn left onto HI-32 W, and then right onto HI-30 W to reach the plantation.

GPS Coordinates: 20.8491053° N, 156.5067995° W

Best Time to Visit: Morning to mid-afternoon for guided tours and optimal light for photos.

Pass/Permit/Fees: Free to enter; tram tours and certain activities may have fees.

Did You Know? The plantation features over 60 acres of cultivated land, showcasing tropical plants and flowers unique to the islands.

Website:
http://www.mauitropicalplantation.com/?utm_source=TripAdvisor&utm_medium=MTP

OAHU

HALEIWA

Laniakea Beach

Find your sense of wonder at Laniakea Beach, located at 61-574 Pohaku Loa Way in Haleiwa, Oahu. This stunning beach is renowned for its frequent green sea turtle sightings, offering visitors a unique opportunity to observe these majestic creatures up close. Also known as Turtle Beach, Laniakea boasts a beautiful stretch of sand perfect for sunbathing and leisurely walks. The clear waters provide excellent conditions for snorkeling and swimming, making it an ideal spot for family fun and marine exploration.

Location: 574, 61-574 Pohaku Loa Way, Haleiwa, Oahu, HI 96712

Closest City or Town: Haleiwa, Oahu

How to Get There: From Haleiwa town, head east on Kamehameha Highway and turn onto Pohaku Loa Way to reach the beach parking area.

GPS Coordinates: 21.6187696° N, 158.0854313° W

Best Time to Visit: Morning for turtle sightings and calm waters.

Pass/Permit/Fees: Free to visit.

Did You Know? Laniakea Beach is one of the best places in Oahu to spot Hawaiian green sea turtles basking on the sand.

Website: https://www.hawaiiactivities.com/travelguide/laniakea-beach/

Sunset Beach Park

Find your sense of adventure at Sunset Beach Park, a legendary surf destination located in Haleiwa, Oahu. This stunning beach is renowned for its towering waves in the winter, attracting surfers from around the world, and offering calm, inviting waters perfect for swimming and snorkeling in the summer. Located along the North Shore, visitors can experience breathtaking sunsets that paint the sky in hues of orange and pink. Activities include surfing, bodyboarding, and sunbathing on the golden sands. The unique feature of Sunset Beach is the chance to witness world-class surf competitions and bask in the natural beauty of Oahu's rugged coast.

Location: 59-104 Kamehameha Hwy, Haleiwa, Oahu, HI 96712-9728

Closest City or Town: Haleiwa, Oahu, HI

How to Get There: From Honolulu, take the H-1 to H-2 freeway, then the Kamehameha Hwy (Route 99) to the North Shore.

GPS Coordinates: 21.6742067° N, 158.0390432° W

Best Time to Visit: Winter for surfing, summer for swimming and snorkeling.

Pass/Permit/Fees: Free to visit.

Did You Know? Sunset Beach is one of the premier spots in the world for big wave surfing, with waves reaching up to 30 feet in height during peak season.

Website: https://www.gohawaii.com/treks/oahu/sunset-beach.html

Waimea Bay

Get ready for an oceanic adventure at Waimea Bay, a pristine beach located in Haleiwa, Oahu. Famous for its enormous surf during the winter months, Waimea Bay draws thrill-seeking surfers from across the globe to tackle its monstrous waves. During the calmer summer season, the bay transforms into a haven for swimming, snorkeling, and cliff diving. Situated along the scenic North Shore, it provides an excellent spot for picnicking and beachcombing. The unique feature of Waimea Bay is its transformation from a tranquil swimming spot in summer to a surfer's paradise in winter, offering two distinct experiences in one stunning location.

Location: Kamehameha Hwy, Haleiwa, Oahu, HI 96712-1304

Closest City or Town: Haleiwa, Oahu, HI

How to Get There: From Honolulu, take H-1 to H-2 freeway, followed by Route 99 to Route 83 (Kamehameha Hwy) to Waimea Bay.

GPS Coordinates: 21.5571360° N, 157.8764854° W

Best Time to Visit: Winter for surfing, summer for swimming and diving.

Pass/Permit/Fees: Free to visit.

Did You Know? Waimea Bay is home to the Eddie Aikau Big Wave Invitational, held only when waves reach a minimum of 20 feet.

Website: https://www.gohawaii.com/islands/oahu/regions/north-shore/waimea-bay

HONOLULU

Ala Moana Beach Park

Explore paradise with a local twist at Ala Moana Beach Park, an urban oasis located in bustling Honolulu, Oahu. This expansive park features a golden beachfront, lush grassy areas, and shaded picnic spots, making it perfect for relaxation and recreation. Situated on Ala Moana Boulevard, it's a favorite spot for swimming, paddleboarding, and beach volleyball. Enjoy a leisurely stroll along the coastal promenade, or take part in a yoga session on the beach with the stunning Waikiki skyline as your backdrop.

Location: 1201 Ala Moana Blvd, Honolulu, Oahu, HI 96814-4205

Closest City or Town: Honolulu, Oahu

How to Get There: From Waikiki, head west on Ala Moana Boulevard and the park will be on your left after crossing Atkinson Drive.

GPS Coordinates: 21.2899686° N, 157.8476570° W

Best Time to Visit: Throughout the day, but the evenings are fantastic for a sunset picnic.

Pass/Permit/Fees: Free to visit.

Did You Know? Ala Moana Beach Park is one of the few places in Honolulu that offers free parking.

Website: https://www.honolulu.gov/parks/default/park-locations/182-site-dpr-cat/30221-ala-moana-regional-park.html

Aloha Pearl Harbor Tours

Step into history with Aloha Pearl Harbor Tours, offering a deep dive into one of America's most significant historical events. Situated in the heart of Honolulu, this guided tour takes you through the Pearl Harbor National Memorial, the USS Arizona Memorial, and other poignant sites. Located on Lili'uokalani Avenue, it's an enriching experience featuring detailed narratives, interactive exhibits, and historical reenactments. This tour is perfect for history buffs and families eager to learn about the bravery and sacrifice that marked this pivotal moment in history.

Location: 140 Lili'uokalani Ave, Honolulu, HI 96815

Closest City or Town: Honolulu, Hawaii

How to Get There: From Waikiki, head northwest on Kalakaua Avenue, then turn left onto S King Street. Continue straight to arrive at Lili'uokalani Avenue.

GPS Coordinates: 21.2752848° N, 157.8232362° W

Best Time to Visit: Early morning tours are less crowded.

Pass/Permit/Fees: Fees vary; booking in advance is recommended.

Did You Know? The USS Arizona Memorial is built over the remains of the battleship sunk during the attack on Pearl Harbor, serving as a resting place for over 1,000 sailors.

Website: http://alohapearlharbor.com/partners/tripadvisor/offer/

Battleship Missouri Memorial

Embark on a journey through naval history at the Battleship Missouri Memorial, a mighty vessel docked in Pearl Harbor, Oahu. This historic battleship once served in World War II, the Korean War, and the Persian Gulf War, and now stands as a monument to peace and justice. Located on Cowpens Street, the Mighty Mo invites visitors to explore her decks, hear firsthand accounts from wartime veterans, and witness where the Japanese surrender was signed. It's an experience that fosters respect and admiration for those who have served.

Location: 63 Cowpens St, Honolulu, Oahu, HI 96818-5006

Closest City or Town: Honolulu, Oahu

How to Get There: From Honolulu, take HI-92 west to Arizona Memorial Place. Follow signs for the Battleship Missouri Memorial.

GPS Coordinates: 21.3621169° N, 157.9534244° W

Best Time to Visit: Morning to mid-afternoon, for guided tours and cooler weather.

Pass/Permit/Fees: Admission fees apply; see their website for details.

Did You Know? The Mighty Mo was the site of the official Japanese surrender that ended World War II.

Website: https://www.ussmissouri.org/

Bishop Museum

Immerse yourself in Hawaiian culture and history at the Bishop Museum, located in Honolulu, Oahu. Founded in 1889, this museum boasts the world's largest collection of Polynesian cultural artifacts and natural history specimens. Situated on Bernice Street, it offers engaging exhibits ranging from ancient Hawaiian artifacts to contemporary island science. Enjoy planetarium shows, explore fossils, or participate in interactive workshops that provide a deep dive into Hawaii's rich heritage.

Location: 1525 Bernice Street, Honolulu, Oahu, HI 96817-2704

Closest City or Town: Honolulu, Oahu

How to Get There: From downtown Honolulu, drive north on Nuuanu Avenue, then turn right onto Bernice Street.

GPS Coordinates: 21.3329195° N, 157.8706127° W

Best Time to Visit: Weekdays to avoid the weekend rush.

Pass/Permit/Fees: Entry fees apply; purchase tickets online for discounts.

Did You Know? The Bishop Museum was established in honor of Princess Bernice Pauahi Bishop, the last descendant of the Kamehameha Dynasty.

Website: http://www.bishopmuseum.org/

Diamond Head Crater

Find your sense of adventure at Diamond Head Crater, an iconic landmark located in Honolulu, Hawaii. Hike up the prehistoric volcanic crater for panoramic views of Waikiki Beach and the glistening Pacific Ocean. This moderately challenging trail takes you through tunnels and up steep stairs, offering a rewarding vista at the summit. Beyond its natural beauty, Diamond Head is steeped in history, having once served as a military lookout. The unique combination of geological wonder and historical significance makes this a must-visit for hikers and history buffs alike.

Location: 757V+CV Honolulu, Hawaii, Stati Uniti

Closest City or Town: Honolulu, Hawaii

How to Get There: From downtown Honolulu, take Diamond Head Road and follow signs to the park entrance.

GPS Coordinates: 21.2625529° N, 157.8058607° W

Best Time to Visit: Early morning to beat the heat and crowds.

Pass/Permit/Fees: Entrance fee applies; visit the website for current rates.

Did You Know? The summit of Diamond Head provides a 360-degree view of the surrounding island, including parts of the Southeast Oahu coastline.

Website: https://dlnr.hawaii.gov/dsp/parks/oahu/diamond-head-state-monument/

Diamond Head State Monument

Embark on a geological and historical journey at Diamond Head State Monument, located in Honolulu, Oahu. This world-famous volcanic tuff cone offers visitors a chance to explore the ancient crater and enjoy breathtaking views from its summit. The 0.8-mile hike features steep stairways, dark tunnels, and a rewarding lookout point. Diamond Head is not just a natural wonder; it was also a strategic military site in the early 1900s. Its unique blend of natural beauty and historical context makes it a fascinating destination for all types of adventurers.

Location: Diamond Head Road 18th Ave., Honolulu, Oahu, HI 96815

Closest City or Town: Honolulu, Oahu

How to Get There: From Waikiki, drive along Kalakaua Avenue and turn onto Diamond Head Road, which leads directly to the park.

GPS Coordinates: 21.2674228° N, 157.7997989° W

Best Time to Visit: Visit early for cooler temperatures and fewer tourists.

Pass/Permit/Fees: Entrance fee required; check the website for up-to-date fees.

Did You Know? Diamond Head State Monument was designated a National Natural Landmark in 1968.

Website: https://dlnr.hawaii.gov/dsp/parks/oahu/diamond-head-state-monument/

Hanauma Bay Nature Preserve

Dive into the aquatic splendor of Hanauma Bay Nature Preserve, a protected marine life conservation area in Honolulu, Oahu. Famous for its crystal-clear waters and vibrant coral reefs, this bay offers spectacular snorkeling and swimming opportunities. Visitors can explore an underwater paradise teeming with colorful fish and other marine creatures. Originally a volcanic crater, Hanauma Bay's unique shape creates a calm and welcoming environment for snorkelers of all levels. This underwater haven is an ideal spot for marine life enthusiasts and families seeking a safe beach experience.

Location: 100 Hanauma Bay Rd, Honolulu, Oahu, HI 96825-2005

Closest City or Town: Honolulu, Oahu

How to Get There: From Waikiki, take the H1 Freeway eastbound, follow signs to Hanauma Bay.

GPS Coordinates: 21.2688327° N, 157.6931641° W

Best Time to Visit: Early morning to avoid crowds and enjoy calm waters.

Pass/Permit/Fees: Entry fee required; visit the website for details.

Did You Know? Visitors to Hanauma Bay must watch an educational video to learn about the bay's fragile ecosystem and how to protect it.

Website: http://www.honolulu.gov/parks-hbay/home.html

Honolulu Museum of Art

Immerse yourself in the cultural richness of Honolulu Museum of Art, located in the heart of Honolulu, Oahu. This world-class museum boasts an extensive collection of art spanning centuries and continents, from Asian masterpieces to contemporary Hawaiian works. Stroll through the elegant galleries, enjoy the serene courtyards, and participate in diverse art workshops and lectures. The Honolulu Museum of Art stands out for its dedication to both global and local art, making it a cultural treasure trove for art lovers.

Location: 900 S Beretania St, Honolulu, Oahu, HI 96814-1495

Closest City or Town: Honolulu, Oahu

How to Get There: From Waikiki, take Kalakaua Avenue, turn left on South Beretania Street.

GPS Coordinates: 21.3039364° N, 157.8484556° W

Best Time to Visit: Year-round, with special events and exhibitions throughout the year.

Pass/Permit/Fees: Admission fees apply; visit the website for current rates.

Did You Know? The museum's Doris Duke Theatre regularly screens international films and documentaries.

Website: http://www.honolulumuseum.org/

Iolani Palace

Step back in time at Iolani Palace, the former royal residence located in Honolulu, Oahu. As the only official state residence of royalty in the United States, the palace offers a captivating glimpse into Hawaii's monarchical past. Visitors can tour the opulent halls, adorned with historical artifacts and sumptuous décor. Discover the intriguing stories of Hawaii's last reigning monarchs and the palace's role in Hawaiian history. The unique historical significance and architectural grandeur make Iolani Palace a must-see for history enthusiasts.

Location: 364 S King St, Honolulu, Oahu, HI 96813-2900

Closest City or Town: Honolulu, Oahu

How to Get There: From Waikiki, take Ala Wai Boulevard to South King Street.

GPS Coordinates: 21.3067572° N, 157.8587697° W

Best Time to Visit: Any time of year, with fewer crowds during weekdays.

Pass/Permit/Fees: Entry fee required; visit the website for tickets and tours.

Did You Know? Iolani Palace features the first flushing toilets and electric lights in Hawaii.

Website: http://www.iolanipalace.org/

Izumo Taishakyo Mission of Hawaii

Find your spiritual tranquility at the Izumo Taishakyo Mission of Hawaii, an authentic Shinto shrine nestled in the heart of Honolulu, Oahu. Reflect on your journey as you wander through the peaceful grounds, participate in traditional rituals, and soak in the serene ambiance of this sacred space. This historic shrine, founded in 1906, offers a unique opportunity to experience Japanese religious culture outside of Japan. Immerse yourself in the calming beauty, engage in meditation, or attend a special ceremony to feel the deep connection between history and spirituality.

Location: 215 N Kukui St, Honolulu, Oahu, HI 96817-3951

Closest City or Town: Honolulu, Oahu

How to Get There: From downtown Honolulu, take Nuuanu Avenue north and turn right onto N Kukui Street. The shrine is located on the left.

GPS Coordinates: 21.3157092° N, 157.8609925° W

Best Time to Visit: Year-round, with fewer crowds during weekdays.

Pass/Permit/Fees: Free to visit; donations appreciated.

Did You Know? The Izumo Taishakyo Mission is one of the oldest Shinto shrines in Hawaii, symbolizing peace and cultural exchange.

Website: https://www.izumotaishahawaii.com/

King Kamehameha Statue

Feel the power of history as you gaze upon the imposing King Kamehameha Statue, a symbol of Hawaiian unity and strength located in downtown Honolulu. This iconic statue commemorates King Kamehameha I, the great monarch who unified the Hawaiian Islands in the early 19th century. Standing proudly in front of Ali'iolani

Hale, it offers a connection to the rich cultural heritage of Hawaii. Visitors can admire the detailed craftsmanship of the statue, learn about the king's legacy, and snap photos with this significant landmark.

Location: 417 S King St, Honolulu, Oahu, HI 96813-2943

Closest City or Town: Honolulu, Oahu

How to Get There: From Waikiki, drive west on Kalakaua Avenue and turn onto King Street. The statue is located in front of Ali'iolani Hale.

GPS Coordinates: 21.3057277° N, 157.8596457° W

Best Time to Visit: Morning or early evening for less crowded photo opportunities.

Pass/Permit/Fees: Free to visit.

Did You Know? Every June 11th, King Kamehameha Day, the statue is draped with flower leis in a colorful and festive ceremony.

Website:
https://www.gohawaii.com/islands/oahu/regions/honolulu/king-kamehameha-statue

Koko Crater Arch Trail

Embark on an adventurous hike along the Koko Crater Arch Trail, a thrilling path located in Honolulu, Oahu. This moderate-to-challenging trail offers breathtaking coastal views, steep inclines, and a rewarding natural arch at the summit. Climbing through rugged terrain, hikers can enjoy panoramic vistas of the sparkling Pacific Ocean and the island's stunning landscapes. This trail is not only a test of endurance but also a celebration of Oahu's raw, untouched beauty.

Location: 7968-8456 Kalaniana'ole Hwy, Honolulu, HI 96825

Closest City or Town: Honolulu, Oahu

How to Get There: From Honolulu, take Kalaniana'ole Highway east; the trailhead is located near the Koko Crater Botanical Garden entrance.

GPS Coordinates: 21.2806776° N, 157.6785362° W

Best Time to Visit: Early morning for cooler temperatures and fewer hikers.

Pass/Permit/Fees: Free to hike.

Did You Know? The arch is a natural rock formation created by volcanic activity millions of years ago.

Website: http://www.honolulu.gov/cms-dpr-menu/site-dpr-sitearticles/572-koko-crater-botanical-garden.html

Lyon Arboretum

Explore the lush botanical wonderland of Lyon Arboretum, a tranquil oasis located in the verdant Manoa Valley in Honolulu, Oahu. Wander through over 200 acres of tropical plants, serene trails, and picturesque gardens. As part of the University of Hawaii, this extensive research facility educates visitors on botany and conservation. The arboretum's vast collections of Hawaiian flora make it a haven for nature lovers and plant enthusiasts alike.

Location: 3860 Manoa Rd University of Hawaii-Manoa, Honolulu, Oahu, HI 96822-1198

Closest City or Town: Honolulu, Oahu

How to Get There: From downtown Honolulu, drive north on Manoa Road following signs to the University of Hawaii; the arboretum is located at the end of the road.

GPS Coordinates: 21.3329710° N, 157.8015390° W

Best Time to Visit: Year-round, with mornings recommended for cooler temperatures and vibrant bird activity.

Pass/Permit/Fees: Entrance fee applies; check the website for details.

Did You Know? Lyon Arboretum is home to a vast collection of native Hawaiian plant species that are found nowhere else in the world.

Website: http://manoa.hawaii.edu/lyon/

Magic Island

Discover the enchanting Magic Island, a man-made peninsula located at the end of Ala Moana Beach Park in Honolulu, Oahu. This idyllic spot is perfect for picnicking, jogging, and enjoying panoramic views of the Waikiki skyline and Diamond Head. Stroll along the paths, relax in shaded areas, or swim in the calm, protected lagoon. Magic Island's beautiful setting creates a serene escape amid the bustling city life, making it a favorite local retreat.

Location: 1201 Ala Moana Blvd At the end of Ala Moana Beach Park, Honolulu, Oahu, HI 96814-4205

Closest City or Town: Honolulu, Oahu

How to Get There: From Waikiki, drive west on Ala Moana Boulevard and continue straight until you reach the park entrance.

GPS Coordinates: 21.2901851° N, 157.8476658° W

Best Time to Visit: Early morning or late afternoon for cooler temperatures and beautiful sunset views.

Pass/Permit/Fees: Free to visit.

Did You Know? Magic Island was originally designed as a resort but was converted into a public park, providing a peaceful haven in urban Honolulu.

Website: https://www.to-hawaii.com/oahu/beaches/magicislandbeach.php

Makapu'u Point Lighthouse Trail

Find your sense of adventure along the Makapu'u Point Lighthouse Trail, offering breathtaking views on the southeastern tip of Oahu, Hawaii. Wander along this scenic hike to marvel at the historic red-roofed lighthouse and panoramic vistas of the Pacific Ocean and nearby islands. Located at the end of Kalaniana'ole Highway, the trail is an easy to moderate hike, perfect for all ages. Enjoy whale watching in winter or simply bask in the stunning natural beauty at any time of year. This trail is renowned for its clear views and perfect photo opportunities, making it a must-visit for nature lovers.

Location: 8751-9057 Kalaniana'ole Hwy, Honolulu, HI 96825

Closest City or Town: Honolulu, Hawaii

How to Get There: From downtown Honolulu, head east on Kalaniana'ole Highway past Hanauma Bay, and follow the signs to the trailhead.

GPS Coordinates: 21.2907538° N, 157.6648669° W

Best Time to Visit: Early morning for cooler temperatures and fewer crowds.

Pass/Permit/Fees: Free to visit.

Did You Know? The lighthouse at Makapu'u Point, built-in 1909, boasts one of the largest lenses in use in the United States.

Website: https://www.alltrails.com/trail/hawaii/oahu/makapu-u-point-lighthouse-trail

Manoa Falls

Immerse yourself in the serene beauty of Manoa Falls, a majestic waterfall located in a lush valley near Honolulu, Hawaii. This easy trail leads you through a verdant rainforest, rich with exotic plants and birdlife, to the scenic 150-foot waterfall. Ideal for nature enthusiasts of all ages, the hike takes you through bamboo groves and winding paths, ending at the stunning cascade. The unique feature of this trail is its lush tropical foliage and serene ambiance, providing a refreshing escape from the city.

Location: 86R2+H4 Honolulu, Hawaii

Closest City or Town: Honolulu, Hawaii

How to Get There: From downtown Honolulu, take Punahou Street and continue on Manoa Road until you reach the trailhead.

GPS Coordinates: 21.3420389° N, 157.7992015° W

Best Time to Visit: Early morning or late afternoon to avoid crowds.

Pass/Permit/Fees: Free to visit; parking fees may apply.

Did You Know? The Manoa Falls Trail was featured in films like Jurassic Park and the TV series Lost due to its lush, prehistoric setting.

Website: https://www.hawaii.com/manoa-falls-trail/

National Memorial Cemetery of the Pacific

Pay your respects at the National Memorial Cemetery of the Pacific, also known as Punchbowl Cemetery, located in Honolulu, Oahu. This solemn and beautifully landscaped site honors the sacrifices of

American armed forces. Wander through the serene grounds and take in the splendid views of Honolulu and Diamond Head. Nestled within a volcanic crater, the cemetery offers a peaceful spot for reflection amidst informative historical markers and stunning memorials.

Location: 2177 Puowaina Dr, Honolulu, Oahu, HI 96813-1729

Closest City or Town: Honolulu, Oahu, Hawaii

How to Get There: From downtown Honolulu, take H-1 and exit at Punchbowl Street, continue north and follow signs to the cemetery.

GPS Coordinates: 21.3130733° N, 157.8426468° W

Best Time to Visit: Visit during daylight hours; the early morning provides a peaceful environment.

Pass/Permit/Fees: Free to visit.

Did You Know? The cemetery is often referred to as Punchbowl because it is located inside the crater of an extinct volcano.

Website: http://www.cem.va.gov/CEMs/nchp/nmcp.asp

Pearl Harbor Aviation Museum

Soar through history at the Pearl Harbor Aviation Museum, situated on Historic Ford Island in Honolulu, Oahu. This remarkable museum tells the story of the Pacific aviation in World War II with a vast collection of aircraft, personal stories, and interactive exhibits. Engage with history as you explore the hangars that survived the December 7, 1941, attack. Learn about the bravery of aviators and the monumental battles that took to the skies.

Location: 319 Lexington Blvd Historic Ford Island, Honolulu, Oahu, HI 96818-5004

Closest City or Town: Honolulu, Oahu, Hawaii

How to Get There: From Honolulu, take H-1 to Nimitz Highway, follow signs to Ford Island, and proceed to the museum.

GPS Coordinates: 21.3597342° N, 157.9618410° W

Best Time to Visit: Morning to avoid crowds and heat.

Pass/Permit/Fees: Admission fees apply; see the website for current rates.

Did You Know? The museum is located in the hangars that still bear shrapnel scars from the Pearl Harbor attack.

Website: http://www.pearlharboraviationmuseum.org/

Pearl Harbor National Memorial

Honor the past at the Pearl Harbor National Memorial, dedicated to preserving the memory of the attack on December 7, 1941. Located in Honolulu, Oahu, this poignant site includes the USS Arizona Memorial, where visitors can pay respects to the fallen sailors resting beneath the waves. The museum and visitor center offer moving exhibits about the day's events and the subsequent World War II battles. This place of remembrance offers a sobering history lesson and a tribute to American resilience.

Location: 1 Arizona Memorial Place, Honolulu, Oahu, HI 96818

Closest City or Town: Honolulu, Oahu, Hawaii

How to Get There: From downtown Honolulu, take the H-1 Freeway to Exit 15A and follow signs to the memorial.

GPS Coordinates: 21.3675985° N, 157.9388580° W

Best Time to Visit: Early morning when the site is less crowded.

Pass/Permit/Fees: Free to visit; reservations recommended.

Did You Know? The USS Arizona Memorial sits atop the sunken battleship, honoring more than 1,100 sailors who lost their lives.

Website: https://www.nps.gov/valr/pearl-harbor-national-memorial.htm

Puu Ualakaa State Park

Find tranquility and panoramic views at Puu Ualakaa State Park, a serene oasis perched atop Tantalus Drive in Honolulu, Oahu. This park offers some of the best scenic vistas of the city skyline and the lush valleys below. Located along Round Top Drive, it's the perfect spot for picnicking, hiking, and photography. The Tantalus-Round Top

Drive Scenic Byway is a journey through tropical greenery that makes this destination truly unique.

Location: 2760 Round Top Drive, Honolulu, Oahu, HI 96822

Closest City or Town: Honolulu, Oahu

How to Get There: From downtown Honolulu, head northwest on Ward Avenue, turn left onto Round Top Drive, and follow it to the park.

GPS Coordinates: 21.3125434° N, 157.8249362° W

Best Time to Visit: Late afternoon for stunning sunset views.

Pass/Permit/Fees: Free to visit.

Did You Know? Puu Ualakaa State Park is one of the few places in Oahu where you can capture a full panorama of Honolulu cityscape against the backdrop of the Pacific Ocean.

Website: http://dlnr.hawaii.gov/dsp/parks/oahu/puu-ualakaa-state-wayside/

Queen Emma Summer Palace

Step into the regal past at Queen Emma Summer Palace, a historic retreat located in Honolulu, Oahu. This beautifully preserved home was the summer retreat of Queen Emma of Hawaii. Nestled along Pali Highway, visitors can explore the royal residence, adorned with charming period furnishings and authentic artifacts. The unique aspect of this destination is its fascinating insight into the Hawaiian monarchy and lush surrounding gardens.

Location: 2913 Pali Hwy, Honolulu, Oahu, HI 96817-1417

Closest City or Town: Honolulu, Oahu

How to Get There: From downtown Honolulu, drive northwest on Pali Highway; the palace is on the left side.

GPS Coordinates: 21.3360577° N, 157.8391509° W

Best Time to Visit: Year-round, with historical tours available daily.

Pass/Permit/Fees: Entry fees apply; visit the website for more details.

Did You Know? Queen Emma Summer Palace is also known as Hānaiakamalama, meaning The Foster Child of the Moon.

Website: http://queenemmasummerpalace.org/

Shangri La

Discover the exquisite blend of arts and culture at Shangri La, a spectacular estate situated in Honolulu, Oahu. Once the home of Doris Duke, this luxurious mansion now serves as a museum for Islamic art, culture, and design. Located on Papu Circle, visitors can marvel at Duke's impressive collection of exotic artifacts, pristine architecture, and breathtaking ocean views. The unique feature of Shangri La is its stunning Moorish design juxtaposed against the tropical Hawaiian landscape.

Location: 4055 Papu Cir, Honolulu, Oahu, HI 96816-4850

Closest City or Town: Honolulu, Oahu

How to Get There: From downtown Honolulu, take Diamond Head Road to Papu Circle and follow the signs to Doris Duke's Shangri La.

GPS Coordinates: 21.2570987° N, 157.7949963° W

Best Time to Visit: Year-round, with guided tours available.

Pass/Permit/Fees: Tour fees apply; book tickets in advance online.

Did You Know? Doris Duke, the wealthy American heiress and philanthropist, handpicked many of the artifacts during her extensive travels across the Middle East and Asia.

Website: http://shangrilahawaii.org/

St. Augustine by the Sea

Experience a blend of spiritual peace and history at St. Augustine by the Sea, a historic church located in the heart of Waikiki, Honolulu, Oahu. This beautiful church offers a serene sanctuary with a rich history dating back to the early 20th century. Situated on Ohua Avenue, it's a place where visitors can attend mass, admire the stunning stained-glass windows, and arrive for peaceful contemplation against the backdrop of ocean views.

Location: 130 Ohua Avenue, Honolulu, Oahu, HI 96815-3642

Closest City or Town: Honolulu, Oahu

How to Get There: From Waikiki, head south on Kalakaua Avenue and turn left onto Ohua Avenue.

GPS Coordinates: 21.2736795° N, 157.8230905° W

Best Time to Visit: Early morning or late afternoon to avoid the tourist rush.

Pass/Permit/Fees: Free to visit; donations are welcomed.

Did You Know? St. Augustine by the Sea is noted for its remarkable bell tower, which houses the oldest bell in Hawaii.

Website: http://staugustinebythesea.com/

Statue of Duke Kahanamoku

Celebrate the legacy of Hawaii's legendary surfer at the Statue of Duke Kahanamoku, prominently located on Kalakaua Avenue at Kuhio Beach Park in Honolulu, Oahu. This iconic bronze statue pays tribute to Duke Kahanamoku, often regarded as the father of modern surfing. Visitors can snap photos with the statue, bask in the sun on the nearby beach, and absorb the surf culture that Duke represented and popularized.

Location: Kalakaua Ave Kuhio Beach Park, Honolulu, Oahu, HI 96815

Closest City or Town: Honolulu, Oahu

How to Get There: From Waikiki, walk along Kalakaua Avenue towards Kuhio Beach Park.

GPS Coordinates: 21.2755195° N, 157.8253238° W

Best Time to Visit: Anytime, but sunset provides an especially beautiful backdrop.

Pass/Permit/Fees: Free to visit.

Did You Know? Duke Kahanamoku was not only a surfing legend but also an Olympic swimmer with five medals to his name.

Website: http://www.to-hawaii.com/oahu/attractions/dukestatue.php

Tantalus Lookout Puu Ualakaa State Park

Find serenity amid breathtaking views at the Tantalus Lookout in Puu Ualakaa State Park, located in the lush Round Top Forest Reserve of Honolulu, Oahu. This park offers some of the best scenic vistas of the city skyline and the verdant valleys below. Enjoy a picnic, take a leisurely hike, or capture stunning photographs of the panoramic views encompassing Honolulu and the Pacific Ocean. This lookout is a perfect retreat for those seeking tranquility and natural beauty.

Location: Nutridge St Round Top Forest Reserve, Honolulu, Oahu, HI 96822

Closest City or Town: Honolulu, Oahu

How to Get There: From downtown Honolulu, head northwest on Ward Avenue, turn left onto Round Top Drive, and follow it to the park.

GPS Coordinates: 21.3134333° N, 157.8228472° W

Best Time to Visit: Late afternoon for stunning sunset views.

Pass/Permit/Fees: Free to visit.

Did You Know? Puu Ualakaa State Park is one of the few places in Oahu where you can capture a full panorama of Honolulu's cityscape against the backdrop of the Pacific Ocean.

Website: http://dlnr.hawaii.gov/dsp/parks/oahu/puu-ualakaa-state-wayside/

US Army Museum of Hawaii

Dive into the rich military history of the Pacific at the US Army Museum of Hawaii, nestled in the historical Battery Randolph on Kalia Road, Honolulu, Oahu. This museum offers fascinating exhibits on Hawaiian military history from ancient times through World War II and the Vietnam War. Explore artifacts, uniforms, and weapons that tell the stories of bravery and sacrifice. The museum's unique features and interactive displays make it a must-visit for history enthusiasts of all ages.

Location: 2131 Kalia Rd, Honolulu, Oahu, HI 96815-1936

Closest City or Town: Honolulu, Oahu

How to Get There: From Waikiki, head west on Kalakaua Avenue, turn right onto Kalia Road, and the museum is on your left.

GPS Coordinates: 21.2788697° N, 157.8333125° W

Best Time to Visit: Late morning or early afternoon.

Pass/Permit/Fees: Free to visit.

Did You Know? The museum is housed in Battery Randolph, part of the coastal fortifications built in 1909 to protect Oahu from attack.

Website: http://www.hiarmymuseumsoc.org/

USS Arizona Memorial

Pay your respects at the USS Arizona Memorial, a solemn and poignant tribute to the sailors who lost their lives during the attack on Pearl Harbor. Located in Honolulu, Oahu, this memorial is built over the remains of the sunken battleship USS Arizona. Learn about the events of December 7, 1941, through moving exhibits and poignant narratives. This historic site offers a somber yet enriching experience that honors American resilience and sacrifice.

Location: 1 Arizona Memorial Place, Honolulu, Oahu, HI 96818

Closest City or Town: Honolulu, Oahu

How to Get There: From downtown Honolulu, take the H-1 Freeway to Exit 15A and follow signs to the memorial.

GPS Coordinates: 21.3647161° N, 157.9499020° W

Best Time to Visit: Early morning when the site is less crowded.

Pass/Permit/Fees: Free to visit; reservations recommended.

Did You Know? The USS Arizona Memorial sits atop the sunken battleship, honoring more than 1,100 sailors who lost their lives.

Website: http://www.nps.gov/valr/index.htm

USS Bowfin Submarine Museum & Park

Experience the underwater world of the USS Bowfin Submarine Museum & Park, an immersive destination located at Pearl Harbor in Honolulu, Oahu. Tour the historic submarine, known as the Pearl

Harbor Avenger, and explore the engaging museum exhibits detailing the history of submarine warfare. The park also features a memorial to the 52 U.S. submarines lost during World War II. This site provides an educational and interactive experience for visitors of all ages.

Location: 11 Arizona Memorial Dr, Honolulu, Oahu, HI 96818-3104

Closest City or Town: Honolulu, Oahu

How to Get There: From Honolulu, take H-1 to the airport exit and follow signs for the Arizona Memorial.

GPS Coordinates: 21.3687502° N, 157.9395017° W

Best Time to Visit: Morning for cooler temperatures and fewer crowds.

Pass/Permit/Fees: Admission fees apply; see the website for details.

Did You Know? The USS Bowfin was launched one year after the attack on Pearl Harbor and is credited with sinking 44 enemy ships during its wartime service.

Website: http://www.bowfin.org/

Waikiki Aquarium

Dive into the marine wonders at the Waikiki Aquarium, located on Kalākaua Avenue in Waikiki, Honolulu, Oahu. Established in 1904, this aquarium houses a diverse array of marine life, including colorful coral reefs, native Hawaiian fish, and endangered monk seals. Interactive exhibits and educational programs make it a fun and informative destination for families and ocean enthusiasts alike. The unique blend of scientific research and public education offers visitors an engaging experience in the world of marine biology.

Location: 2777 Kalākaua Avenue Waikiki, Honolulu, Oahu, HI 96815-4027

Closest City or Town: Honolulu, Oahu

How to Get There: From Waikiki, drive southeast on Kalakaua Avenue; the aquarium will be on your right.

GPS Coordinates: 21.2657981° N, 157.8216482° W

Best Time to Visit: Morning to mid-afternoon for the best lighting and to avoid potential rainy weather.

Pass/Permit/Fees: Admission fees apply; visit the website for current rates.

Did You Know? The Waikiki Aquarium is the second oldest public aquarium in the United States.

Website: http://www.waikikiaquarium.org/

Waikiki Beach

Find your ultimate paradise at Waikiki Beach, an iconic stretch of golden sand located in the heart of Honolulu, Oahu. This legendary beach offers endless opportunities for sunbathing, swimming, surfing, and people-watching, making it a hub of activity day and night. Located near the bustling resort area, Waikiki Beach is a must-visit for those seeking both relaxation and adventure in one stunning locale. Whether you're catching the perfect wave or lounging under a palm tree, Waikiki Beach encapsulates the quintessential Hawaiian experience.

Location: 2005 Kalia Road Hilton Hawaiian Village Waikiki Beach Resort, Honolulu, Oahu, HI 96815

Closest City or Town: Honolulu, Oahu

How to Get There: From downtown Honolulu, head east on Ala Moana Boulevard, then turn onto Kalakaua Avenue. Waikiki Beach is accessible across multiple entry points.

GPS Coordinates: 21.2823950° N, 157.8375350° W

Best Time to Visit: Early morning or late afternoon for fewer crowds and stunning sunrise/sunset views.

Pass/Permit/Fees: Free to visit; rental fees for surfboards and other equipment.

Did You Know? Waikiki Beach was originally a retreat for Hawaiian royalty before it became a world-famous tourist destination.

Website: https://www.gohawaii.com/islands/oahu/things-to-do/beaches/waikiki-beach

KAHUKU

Kahuku Farms

Delight in the flavors of Hawaii at Kahuku Farms, a family-owned farm located on Oahu's North Shore. Here, visitors can enjoy farm tours, sample fresh produce, and savor delicious farm-to-table meals at the café. Set against the scenic backdrop of Kahuku's lush hills, the farm offers a unique insight into sustainable agriculture and the cultivation of tropical crops like papayas, bananas, and cacao. It's a perfect blend of nature, education, and culinary delight, making Kahuku Farms a must-visit destination for food lovers and nature enthusiasts.

Location: 56-800 Kamehameha Hwy, Kahuku, Oahu, HI 96731-2302

Closest City or Town: Kahuku, Oahu

How to Get There: From Honolulu, take H1-W to H2-N, then follow Kamehameha Highway to the farm.

GPS Coordinates: 21.6831502° N, 157.9603655° W

Best Time to Visit: Morning to early afternoon for farm tours and fresh produce.

Pass/Permit/Fees: Tour fees apply; check their website for details.

Did You Know? Kahuku Farms has been sustainably cultivating its land for over 100 years, passed down through generations.

Website: http://www.kahukufarms.com/"

Turtle Bay Beach

Experience tranquility and adventure at Turtle Bay Beach, located on the scenic North Shore of Oahu in Kahuku. This captivating beach offers pristine sands, clear waters, and excellent conditions for surfing, swimming, and paddleboarding. Nature enthusiasts will love snorkeling in the coral-rich waters, where Hawaiian green sea turtles can often be spotted. Turtle Bay is a haven for beach lovers and outdoor adventurers looking to immerse themselves in the natural beauty of Hawaii's coastline.

Location: 57-35 Kuilima Dr, Kahuku, HI 96731

Closest City or Town: Kahuku, Hawaii

How to Get There: From Honolulu, take H-1 West to H-2 North, then follow the signs for Kamehameha Highway (H-83) to Turtle Bay Resort.

GPS Coordinates: 21.7046947° N, 157.9989154° W

Best Time to Visit: Early morning or late afternoon for fewer crowds and gentle surf.

Pass/Permit/Fees: Free to visit.

Did You Know? Turtle Bay Beach was featured in the film "Forgetting Sarah Marshall," making it a popular spot among movie buffs.

Website: https://www.hawaii-guide.com/oahu/beaches/turtle-beach

KAILUA

Kailua Beach Park

Find your perfect beach day at Kailua Beach Park, a stunning destination on the windward side of Oahu, known for its soft white sands and turquoise waters. This beach park offers endless opportunities for water sports, such as kayaking, windsurfing, and paddleboarding. The park's amenities, including picnic areas and restrooms, make it family-friendly and ideal for a full day of fun in the sun. Kailua Beach is the epitome of the idyllic Hawaiian beach experience.

Location: 526 Kawailoa Road, Kailua, Oahu, HI 96734

Closest City or Town: Kailua, Hawaii

How to Get There: From Honolulu, take the Pali Highway (HI-61) to Kailua Road and follow Kawailoa Road to the beach park.

GPS Coordinates: 21.3973960° N, 157.7272179° W

Best Time to Visit: Morning to early afternoon for optimal weather and fewer crowds.

Pass/Permit/Fees: Free to visit.

Did You Know? Kailua Beach has been consistently ranked as one of the best beaches in the United States.

Website: http://www.facebook.com/gokailuabeach

Lanikai Beach

Discover paradise at Lanikai Beach, a picturesque stretch of sand in Kailua, offering calm waters and spectacular views of the Mokulua Islands. This beach is perfect for swimming, kayaking, and sunbathing. Its powdery white sand and crystal-clear water make it an ideal spot for a tranquil beach day. Captivating sunrise scenes and peaceful surroundings make Lanikai Beach an unforgettable destination for all visitors.

Location: 97VM+6Q Kailua, Hawaii

Closest City or Town: Kailua, Hawaii

How to Get There: From Honolulu, take the Pali Highway (HI-61) to Kailua, then follow Aalapapa Drive to Mokulua Drive.

GPS Coordinates: 21.3925378° N, 157.7151208° W

Best Time to Visit: Early morning for calm seas and stunning sunrises.

Pass/Permit/Fees: Free to visit.

Did You Know? The name Lanikai means Heavenly Sea in Hawaiian, perfectly describing its serene beauty.

Website: http://www.best-of-oahu.com/Lanikai-Beach-Oahu-Hawaii.html

Lanikai Pillbox Trail

Embark on an exhilarating hike up the Lanikai Pillbox Trail, offering panoramic views of Kailua's coastline and the sparkling Pacific Ocean. The trail leads to historic World War II pillboxes, making it a hike infused with both natural beauty and history. Located in Lanikai, this moderate trail is popular for sunrise hikes, offering breathtaking vistas and photo opportunities. Adventurers and nature lovers alike will find this trail both challenging and rewarding.

Location: 265 Kaelepulu Dr, Kailua, Oahu, HI 96734-3312

Closest City or Town: Kailua, Hawaii

How to Get There: From Kailua, drive southeast on Lanikai Avenue to Kaelepulu Drive, where the trailhead is located.

GPS Coordinates: 21.3901479° N, 157.7194376° W

Best Time to Visit: Early morning for cooler temperatures and a beautiful sunrise.

Pass/Permit/Fees: Free to hike.

Did You Know? The trail is officially known as the Kaiwa Ridge Trail but is locally referred to as the Pillbox Hike due to the present bunkers.

Website: https://www.facebook.com/lanikaipillbox/

KANEOHE

Byodo-In Temple

Find tranquility and spiritual peace at the Byodo-In Temple, a stunning replica of Japan's ancient Byodo-In Temple in Uji, located in Kaneohe, Oahu. Nestled at the foot of the Ko'olau Mountains, this Buddhist temple offers a serene retreat with beautifully landscaped gardens, koi ponds, and meditation areas. Visitors can ring the sacred bell for good fortune, admire the grand statue of Buddha, and wander through the lush surroundings. The temple's architectural beauty and peaceful ambiance make it a perfect spot for reflection and relaxation.

Location: 47-200 Kahekili Hwy, Kaneohe, Oahu, HI 96744-4562

Closest City or Town: Kaneohe, Oahu

How to Get There: From Honolulu, take HI-83 north and turn onto Kahekili Highway; the temple is located within the Valley of the Temples Memorial Park.

GPS Coordinates: 21.4307074° N, 157.8322517° W

Best Time to Visit: Morning for a peaceful atmosphere and fewer crowds.

Pass/Permit/Fees: Entrance fee applies; visit the website for details.

Did You Know? Byodo-In Temple was built in 1968 to commemorate the 100th anniversary of the first Japanese immigrants to Hawaii.

Website: http://www.byodo-in.com/

Hoomaluhia Botanical Gardens

Discover the lush paradise of Hoomaluhia Botanical Gardens, a tranquil oasis nestled in Kaneohe, Oahu. Wander through verdant landscapes featuring tropical plants from around the world. Enjoy serene walks, family picnics, and catch-and-release fishing at the garden's serene lake. This beautifully maintained botanical garden invites visitors to immerse themselves in the natural beauty of Hawaii, complete with breathtaking mountain views. Whether you're an avid botanist or simply seeking relaxation, Hoomaluhia offers a perfect escape into serenity.

Location: 45-680 Luluku Rd, Kaneohe, Oahu, HI 96744-1855

Closest City or Town: Kaneohe, Oahu

How to Get There: From Honolulu, take H-1 W to Likelike Hwy (HI-63 N) toward Kaneohe. Follow signs to Luluku Road and proceed to the gardens.

GPS Coordinates: 21.3866022° N, 157.8045550° W

Best Time to Visit: Early morning for cooler temperatures and fewer crowds.

Pass/Permit/Fees: Free to visit.

Did You Know? The name Hoomaluhia means a place of peace and tranquility in Hawaiian.

Website: https://www.honolulu.gov/parks/hbg.html?id=569:ho

KAPOLEI

Wet 'n' Wild Hawaii

Dive into a day of excitement at Wet 'n' Wild Hawaii, a premier water park located in Kapolei, Oahu. With over 25 rides and attractions, it's the perfect destination for family fun and adventure. Glide down thrilling water slides, float along the lazy river, or relax in a private cabana. The park offers a variety of rides for all ages, from gentle wave pools for the little ones to adrenaline-pumping slides for thrill-seekers.

Location: 400 Farrington Hwy, Kapolei, Oahu, HI 96707-2020

Closest City or Town: Kapolei, Hawaii

How to Get There: From Honolulu, take the H-1 Freeway west to Exit 1A toward Ko Olina, then follow the signs to Wet 'n' Wild Hawaii on Farrington Highway.

GPS Coordinates: 21.3348205° N, 158.0876209° W

Best Time to Visit: Weekdays for shorter lines and less crowds.

Pass/Permit/Fees: Entrance fees apply; check the website for current rates.

Did You Know? Wet 'n' Wild Hawaii is the only water park in Hawaii, providing a unique ocean-themed adventure for visitors.

Website: http://www.wetnwildhawaii.com/

KO OLINA

Ko Olina Lagoons

Find your slice of paradise at Ko Olina Lagoons, a picturesque series of man-made lagoons located in Kapolei, Oahu. These tranquil lagoons offer calm, clear waters perfect for swimming, snorkeling, and paddleboarding. With their pristine beaches and picturesque landscaping, they provide a relaxing and family-friendly environment. Surrounded by luxurious resorts and lush greenery, Ko Olina Lagoons is a serene escape from the hustle and bustle of everyday life.

Location: 8VHH+FG Kapolei, Hawaii, Stati Uniti

Closest City or Town: Kapolei, Oahu

How to Get There: From Honolulu, take the H-1 freeway west to Ko Olina exit 1A, follow the signs to the lagoons.

GPS Coordinates: 21.3286875° N, 158.1211875° W

Best Time to Visit: Morning to early afternoon for fewer crowds and gentle surf.

Pass/Permit/Fees: Free to visit.

Did You Know? The Ko Olina Lagoons are home to a variety of marine life, including tropical fish and sea turtles.

Website: https://koolina.com/destination/lagoons/

LAIE

Laie Hawaii Temple & Visitors' Center

Immerse yourself in serenity at Laie Hawaii Temple & Visitors' Center, a splendid oasis located in Laie, Oahu. This beautiful temple, surrounded by lush gardens and reflective pools, offers guided tours that provide insights into the temple's history and the beliefs of The Church of Jesus Christ of Latter-day Saints. Visitors can stroll through the manicured grounds, learn about Polynesian culture and heritage, and enjoy the peace and tranquility of this sacred site.

Location: 55-600 Naniloa Loop, Laie, Oahu, HI 96762-2202

Closest City or Town: Laie, Oahu

How to Get There: From Honolulu, take H-1 W and HI-83 N. Follow signs to Laie and the temple.

GPS Coordinates: 21.6479298° N, 157.9290069° W

Best Time to Visit: Early morning or evening for a serene experience.

Pass/Permit/Fees: Free to visit.

Did You Know? Laie Hawaii Temple was the first LDS temple built outside the continental United States.

Website: http://www.churchofjesuschrist.org/temples/details/laie-hawaii-temple

NIGHTLIFE IN HONOLULU

The Magical Mystery Show at Hilton Waikiki Beach

Delight in an evening of enchantment at The Magical Mystery Show, hosted at the Hilton Waikiki Beach Hotel. This captivating performance combines classic magic tricks, contemporary illusions, and audience participation, creating an immersive experience that will leave guests spellbound. Located in the heart of Waikiki, the show offers an entertaining escape for families, couples, and solo travelers alike. Prepare to be amazed as world-class magicians dazzle with their craft in an intimate and engaging setting.

Location: 2500 Kuhio Ave, Hilton Waikiki Beach Hotel, Honolulu, Oahu, HI 96815-3671

Closest City or Town: Honolulu, Oahu

How to Get There: From Waikiki, walk or drive to the Hilton Waikiki Beach Hotel located on Kuhio Avenue.

GPS Coordinates: 21.2754450° N, 157.8220021° W

Best Time to Visit: Evening for the showtimes; check the schedule for specific performance times.

Pass/Permit/Fees: Admission fees apply; visit the website for ticket pricing.

Did You Know? The Magical Mystery Show features rotating guest magicians, offering unique performances every time.

Website: https://hotel-magic.com/

Oahu

Halona Blowhole

Witness the awe-inspiring power of nature at Halona Blowhole, a spectacular natural geyser located on the southeastern coast of Oahu. This striking geological feature shoots sea water high into the air through a lava tube, creating a dramatic display each time waves crash into the shore. Situated near Sandy Beach Park, visitors can also enjoy panoramic views of the rugged coastline and explore nearby attractions like the Halona Cove, famously featured in the movie From Here to Eternity.

Location: Kalanian'ole Highway, Oahu, HI 96825

Closest City or Town: Honolulu, Oahu

How to Get There: From Honolulu, take HI-1 East, continue on Kalaniana'ole Highway, and look for signs indicating the Halona Blowhole lookout.

GPS Coordinates: 21.2852719° N, 157.6750544° W

Best Time to Visit: Mid-morning to late afternoon when tides are higher for more impressive blowhole activity.

Pass/Permit/Fees: Free to visit.

Did You Know? Halona, in Hawaiian, means lookout, aptly describing the stunning vistas from this vantage point.

Website: https://www.hawaii.com/halona-blowhole-beach-cove/

North Shore

Embrace the surf culture at Hawaii's North Shore, located on Oahu. Famous for its world-class surf breaks, especially during the winter months, this coastal area attracts surfers from around the globe. Beyond the waves, visitors can explore charming towns like Haleiwa, pristine beaches, and food trucks offering local delights. The North Shore is rich with opportunities for adventure, beachcombing, and basking in the aloha spirit.

Location: 66-160 Kamehameha Hwy, Haleiwa, HI 96712

Closest City or Town: Haleiwa, Oahu

How to Get There: From Honolulu, take H-1 west to H-2 north, then follow signs to the North Shore along Kamehameha Highway.

GPS Coordinates: 21.5890480° N, 158.1021287° W

Best Time to Visit: Winter for surfing; summer for swimming and snorkeling.

Pass/Permit/Fees: Free to visit.

Did You Know? The North Shore's Pipeline is one of the most famous and challenging surf spots in the world.

Website: https://www.gohawaii.com/islands/oahu/regions/north-shore

Nu'uanu Pali

Discover the sweeping vistas and exhilarating winds at Nu'uanu Pali Lookout, a storied cliffside point located on the lush windward coast of Oahu. This historic viewpoint offers panoramic views of the Koolau Mountain Range and Oahu's rugged coastline. Unveil its rich history, where a pivotal battle led by King Kamehameha I took place. Visitors can revel in the scenic beauty, take memorable photos, and feel the powerful trade winds that make this spot unique. Nu'uanu Pali is a must-visit for those seeking both nature's splendor and a touch of Hawaiian history.

Location: 9684+PP Honolulu, Hawaii

Closest City or Town: Honolulu, Hawaii

How to Get There: From downtown Honolulu, take the Pali Highway (HI-61 N) and follow the signs to the lookout.

GPS Coordinates: 21.3666963° N, 157.7935449° W

Best Time to Visit: Early morning or late afternoon for cooler temperatures and fewer crowds.

Pass/Permit/Fees: Free to visit

Did You Know? The name Pali means cliff in Hawaiian, aptly describing this dramatic landscape.

Website:
https://www.gohawaii.com/islands/oahu/regions/windward-coast/nuuanu-pali-lookout

Valley of the Temples

Step into a spiritual retreat at the Valley of the Temples, a serene cemetery nestled against the lush Ko'olau Mountains in Kaneohe, Oahu. The highlight of this tranquil spot is the majestic Byodo-In Temple, a replica of Japan's 950-year-old temple. Visitors can explore the ornate gardens, feed the serene koi in the pond, and meditate amidst the soothing ambiance. With its picturesque scenery and meditative atmosphere, the Valley of the Temples offers a perfect escape into nature and spirituality.

Location: 47-200 Kahekili Hwy, Kaneohe, HI 96744

Closest City or Town: Kaneohe, Oahu

How to Get There: From Honolulu, take H1 west, then northeast on HI-63 N/Likelike Hwy, and follow signs to the Valley of the Temples.

GPS Coordinates: 21.4346887° N, 157.8279229° W

Best Time to Visit: Morning for a peaceful experience and fewer crowds

Pass/Permit/Fees: Entrance fee applies; check the website for details.

Did You Know? The Byodo-In Temple was built in 1968 to commemorate the 100th anniversary of the first Japanese immigrants to Hawaii.

Website: http://www.valley-of-the-temples.com/

PUPUKEA

Banzai Pipeline

Immerse yourself in the thrill of the Banzai Pipeline, a legendary surf spot located in Pupukea on Oahu's North Shore. Famous for its massive, barreling waves, it attracts world-class surfers and spectators alike. During winter months, the waves can reach up to 30 feet, creating an exhilarating spectacle. Along the golden sands, visitors can watch surfers ride the colossal waves or hike the scenic shoreline. Known for its challenging conditions, the Banzai Pipeline is a must-visit for surf enthusiasts and adventure seekers.

Location: 59-355 Ke Nui Road, Pupukea, Oahu, HI 96712

Closest City or Town: Pupukea, Oahu

How to Get There: From Honolulu, take H-1 to H-2 northbound, then follow the Kamehameha Hwy (HI-83) to Pupukea. The beach is well-signposted.

GPS Coordinates: 21.6643828° N, 158.0529971° W

Best Time to Visit: Winter for the best surf conditions.

Pass/Permit/Fees: Free to visit.

Did You Know? The Banzai Pipeline hosts the Billabong Pipe Masters, the final event of the World Surf League's championship tour.

Website: https://lushpalm.com/banzai-pipeline/

Shark's Cove

Dive into an underwater adventure at Shark's Cove, a renowned snorkeling and diving spot located in Haleiwa on Oahu's North Shore. Despite its fearsome name, the cove is a safe haven for snorkelers and divers, offering clear waters teeming with vibrant marine life and intricate rock formations. During the summer months, the calm waters are perfect for underwater exploration, revealing a world of colorful fish and coral. With its serene beauty and flourishing aquatic life, Shark's Cove is a must-visit for nature lovers.

Location: 59694-59698 Kamehameha Hwy, Haleiwa, HI 96712

Closest City or Town: Haleiwa, Oahu

How to Get There: From Honolulu, take H-1 west to H-2 north, and follow the Kamehameha Highway (HI-83) to Haleiwa. The cove is located just past Pūpūkea Beach Park.

GPS Coordinates: 21.6499759° N, 158.0623979° W

Best Time to Visit: Summer months for calm waters.

Pass/Permit/Fees: Free to visit.

Did You Know? Shark's Cove is part of Pūpūkea Marine Life Conservation District, ensuring the protection of its marine environment.

Website: https://www.hawaiimagazine.com/everything-you-need-to-know-about-sharks-cove-oahu/

WAHIAWA

Dole Plantation

Find your sense of wonder at Dole Plantation, a captivating destination located in Wahiawa, Oahu. Delve into the history of pineapple cultivation as you explore the plantation's vast grounds. Take a ride on the Pineapple Express Train Tour, navigate through the Pineapple Garden Maze, and savor Dole's world-famous pineapple ice cream. The plantation offers a delightful mix of fun and education, making it a must-visit for families and food enthusiasts alike. Discover the sweet legacy of James Dole and the fascinating journey of the pineapple industry.

Location: 64-1550 Kamehameha Hwy Dole Plantation, Wahiawa, Oahu, HI 96786-2915

Closest City or Town: Wahiawa, Oahu

How to Get There: From Honolulu, take H-1 West, continue on H-2 North, then take Exit 8 for Wahiawa. Follow signs to the plantation.

GPS Coordinates: 21.5260517° N, 158.0376481° W

Best Time to Visit: Mid-morning to early afternoon for optimal weather and fewer crowds.

Pass/Permit/Fees: Tour fees apply; visit their website for details.

Did You Know? The Pineapple Garden Maze was declared the world's largest maze in 2008 by Guinness World Records.

Website: http://www.doleplantation.com/

Green World Coffee Farms

Immerse yourself in the rich aroma of freshly roasted coffee at Green World Coffee Farms, located in Wahiawa, Oahu. Discover the farm's small-batch roasting process, stroll through picturesque coffee orchards, and sample a variety of coffee blends crafted from beans grown across Hawaii. This inviting farm offers guided tours, a cozy café, and a charming gift shop for all coffee connoisseurs. Embrace the local coffee culture and enjoy a hands-on experience that celebrates the art of coffee making.

Location: 71-101 Kamehameha Hwy, Wahiawa, Oahu, HI 96786-1858

Closest City or Town: Wahiawa, Oahu

How to Get There: From Honolulu, take H-1 West, continue on H-2 North, then take Exit 8 for Wahiawa. Follow signs to the farm.

GPS Coordinates: 21.5129460° N, 158.0412145° W

Best Time to Visit: Early morning to enjoy freshly brewed coffee and guided tours.

Pass/Permit/Fees: Free to visit; fees apply for tours.

Did You Know? Green World Coffee Farms roasts their coffee beans on-site, ensuring the freshest brew for visitors.

Website: http://greenworldcoffeefarm.com/

WAIMANALO

Sea Life Park Hawaii

Dive into an ocean of adventure at Sea Life Park Hawaii, located at stunning Makapuu Point in Waimanalo, Oahu. Watch spectacular dolphin and sea lion shows, get up close with marine life in interactive exhibits, and learn about conservation efforts. This marine theme park and aquarium offer unforgettable experiences with underwater creatures, including sharks and playful penguins. The family-friendly environment ensures fun and education for all ages, set against a breathtaking coastal backdrop.

Location: 41-202 Kalanianaole Hwy Makapuu Point, Waimanalo, Oahu, HI 96795-1820

Closest City or Town: Waimanalo, Oahu

How to Get There: From Honolulu, take HI-1 East, then HI-72 East until you reach Sea Life Park on Kalanianaole Highway.

GPS Coordinates: 21.3137400° N, 157.6635670° W

Best Time to Visit: Morning to early afternoon for fewer crowds and cooler temperatures.

Pass/Permit/Fees: Admission fees apply; check the website for ticket information.

Did You Know? The park's Dolphin Encounter is the only program in Hawaii where you can swim with dolphins in a protected lagoon.

Website: http://www.sealifeparkhawaii.com/

Waimanalo Beach

Relax and rejuvenate at Waimanalo Beach, known for its stunning white sands and gentle waves. Located on the eastern shore of Oahu, this pristine beach offers calm waters ideal for swimming and snorkeling. Enjoy a family picnic under towering ironwood trees or take a leisurely beach walk while basking in the serene aura of the windward coast. With its postcard-perfect landscapes, Waimanalo Beach is a hidden treasure perfect for a peaceful getaway.

Location: 41-305 Kalanianaole Hwy, Waimanalo, Oahu, HI 96795-1806

Closest City or Town: Waimanalo, Oahu

How to Get There: From Honolulu, take HI-1 East and continue onto Kalanianaole Highway towards Waimanalo Beach.

GPS Coordinates: 21.3192097° N, 157.6693432° W

Best Time to Visit: Early morning or late afternoon to avoid the midday heat.

Pass/Permit/Fees: Free to visit.

Did You Know? Waimanalo Beach is one of the longest uninterrupted beaches on Oahu, stretching over 3 miles.

Website: https://www.kailuabeachadventures.com/waimanalo-oahu-beach-guide

MAP

We have devised an interactive map that includes all destinations described in the book.

Upon scanning a provided QR code, a link will be sent to your email, allowing you access to this unique digital feature.

This map is both detailed and user-friendly, marking every location described within the pages of the book. It provides accurate addresses and GPS coordinates for each location, coupled with direct links to the websites of these stunning destinations.

Once you receive your email link and access the interactive map, you'll have an immediate and comprehensive overview of each site's location. This invaluable tool simplifies trip planning and navigation, making it a crucial asset for both first-time visitors and seasoned explorers of Washington.

Scan the following QR or type in the provided link to receive it:

https://jo.my/hawaiibucketlistbonus

You will receive an email with links to access the Interactive Map. If you do not see our email, please look for it in spam or another section of your inbox.

In case you have any problems, you can write us at
TravelBucketList@becrepress.com

Lab. for Planet. Studs.
Cornell U. '05
W4 30 '06

Made in United States
Troutdale, OR
12/19/2024

26964404R00070